THE FAMILY Handyman

ULTIMATE
ONE-DAY
PROJECTS

MORE
STORAGE

PAINTING
SECRETS

CURB
APPEAL

EASY
FIXES

Reader's digest | The Reader's Digest Association Inc.
New York, NY/Montreal

Editorial and Production Team

Vern Johnson, Peggy McDermott, Rick Muscoplat,
Mary Schwender, Marcia Roepke

Photography and Illustrations

Ron Chamberlain, Tom Fenenga, Bruce Kieffer, Mike
Krivit, Don Mannes, Ramon Moreno, Shawn Nielsen,
Doug Oudekerk, Frank Rohrbach III, Eugene Thompson,
Bill Zuehlke

Text, photography and illustrations for *Ultimate One-Day Projects* are based on articles previously published in *The Family Handyman* magazine (2915 Commers Dr., Suite 700, Eagan, MN 55121, familyhandyman.com). For information on advertising in *The Family Handyman* magazine, call (646) 293-6150.

ISBN: 978-1-62145-241-6

THE FAMILY HANDYMAN

Editor in Chief   Ken Collier
Project Editor   Eric Smith
Design & Layout   Diana Boger, Teresa Marrone
Senior Editors   Travis Larson, Gary Wentz
Associate Editors   Jeff Gorton
Administrative Manager   Alice Garrett
Senior Copy Editor   Donna Bierbach
VP, Group Publisher   Russell S. Ellis

Published by Home Service Publications, Inc.,
a subsidiary of The Reader's Digest Association, Inc.

PRINTED IN CHINA

1 2 3 4 5 6 7 8 9 10

A NOTE TO OUR READERS: All do-it-yourself activities involve a degree of risk. Skills, materials, tools and site conditions vary widely. Although the editors have made every effort to ensure accuracy, the reader remains responsible for the selection and use of tools, materials and methods. Always obey local codes and laws, follow manufacturer instructions and observe safety precautions.

Contents

4 Outdoor projects

Bonus Section:
One-Hour Gifts

5 10 big-impact improvements

Special Section: Painting and staining

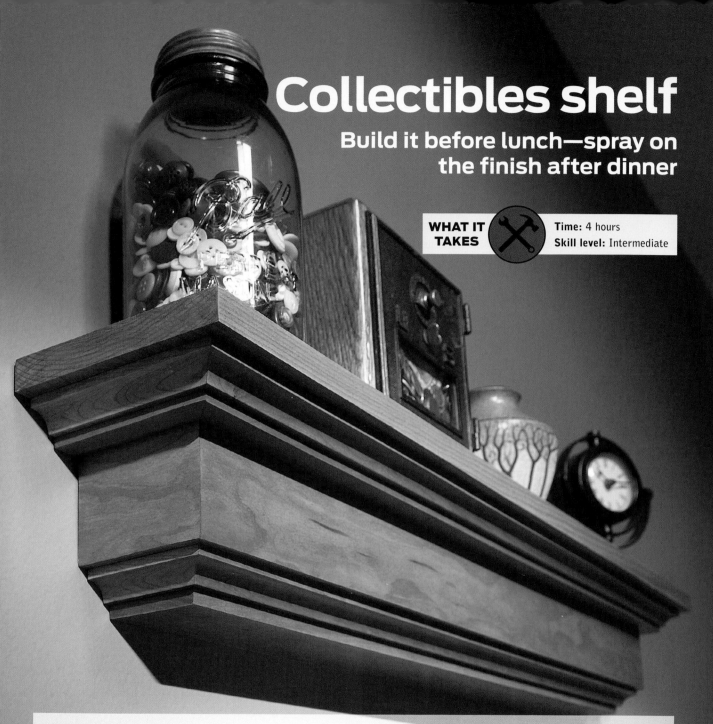

Collectibles shelf
Build it before lunch—spray on the finish after dinner

Sure, you can buy a shelf similar to this one for about $30 at a discount store, but you won't be able to choose the size or finish. We designed ours with a wider top to hold vases and other collectibles, but you can make yours bigger or smaller. Plus, you can finish it to match your room. The shelf is versatile and goes together fast—it would make a great gift. Made from cherry, our shelf cost about $70. It would cost about half that in oak or pine.

Tips for building the shelf

- You'll need a miter saw and a table saw for this project. A finish nailer isn't necessary but is very helpful.
- If you don't have a finish nailer, drill pilot holes for the finish nails to avoid splitting the wood.
- You can use scraps of less expensive lumber for the base (E) and cleats since these aren't visible.
- Glue the parts together. Because you can use fewer nails, you'll have fewer nail holes to fill.

We finished this cherry shelf with a coat of American walnut stain (test the color on a scrap) and three coats of spray satin lacquer. Photo 5 shows how to mount the cleat that supports the shelf. Then you just drop the shelf over the cleat to hang it on the wall.

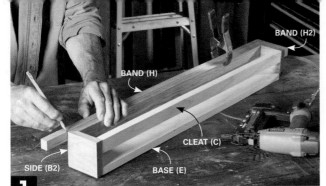

1 **Mark trim parts in place.** Cut the 1-in. band and the cove moldings extra long. Fit the miter on one end, then mark the opposite end for cutting.

Figure A

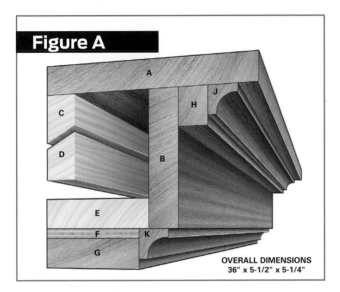

OVERALL DIMENSIONS
36" x 5-1/2" x 5-1/4"

Materials List

ITEM	QTY.
3/4" x 5-1/2" x 8' finish-quality board	1
3/4" x 2-1/2" x 3' finish-quality board	1
1/4" x 30" x 2-1/2" plywood	1
3/4" x 5-1/2" x 3' softwood board	1
3/4" x 3/4" x 8' cove molding	1
Finish nails	

Cutting List

The Cutting List gives finished lengths for the top, front, sides, cleats and bottom. You can cut these to the exact width and length listed and nail them together. The lengths listed for the 3/4-in. x 1-in. bands and the 3/4-in. cove moldings are oversized. You'll mark these pieces in place for an exact fit (Photo 1).

KEY	QTY.	SIZE & DESCRIPTION
A	1	3/4" x 5-1/2" x 36" (top)
B	1	3/4" x 3-1/2" x 32" (front); miter both ends at 45°
B2	2	3/4" x 3-1/2" x 3-1/2" (sides); miter one side
C	1	3/4" x 1-1/4" x 30-1/2" (cleat); 30-degree bevel
D	1	3/4" x 1-1/4" x 30" (cleat); 30-degree bevel
E	1	3/4" x 2-3/4" x 30-1/2" (base)
F	1	1/4" x 2-1/2" x 30" (plywood spacer)
G	1	3/4" x 2-1/2" x 30" (bottom)
H	1	3/4" x 1" x 36" (band); miter both ends to fit
H2	2	3/4" x 1" x 6" (bands); miter both ends to fit
J	1	3/4" x 3/4" x 36" (cove); miter both ends to fit
J2	2	3/4" x 3/4" x 6" (coves); miter both ends to fit
K	1	3/4" x 3/4" x 36" (cove); miter both ends to fit
K2	2	3/4" x 3/4" x 6" (coves); miter both ends to fit

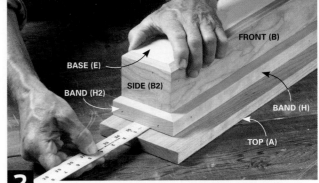

2 **Center the top.** Measure the overhang on each end and adjust the top until it's centered.

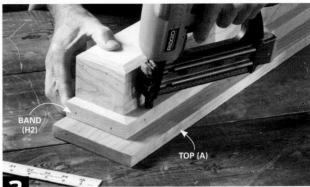

3 **Nail on the top.** Glue the band and nail through it into the top.

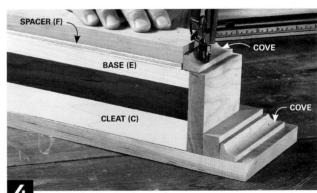

4 **Install the cove moldings.** Add the 1/4-in. spacer and bottom board. Then finish up by fitting and nailing the cove molding.

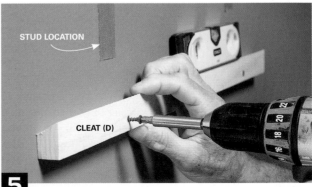

5 **Mount the cleat.** Level the cleat and screw it to the wall. You can locate studs or use drywall anchors.

familyhandyman.com
- For more great shelving projects, search for "shelves."
- Learn how to make perfect miters. Type "miter" into the search box.
- For tips on wood finishing, type "wood finish" into the search box.

Bookcase built by two

Build it in a day with your favorite young woodworker

WHAT IT TAKES **Time:** 1 day
Skill level: Beginner

Here's a simple project that gives you a chance to pass some of your woodworking skills on to the next generation. Any kid will love spending the day with you assembling this bookcase. And by the end of the day, your helper will have hands-on experience with several power tools, plus an attractive bookcase to show off.

The bookcase parts are all standard dimensional lumber that you can find at any home center. The total cost of the knotty pine and other supplies we used was about $40. We joined the shelves and legs with biscuits. If you don't own a biscuit joiner but still want to build this project, you can simply nail or screw the parts together and fill the holes. We used a table saw to cut the 1-1/2-in. square legs from 2x4s and a router with a 45-degree chamfer bit to bevel the edge of the top. If you don't have a table saw or router, you can just use stock 2x2s for the legs and leave the edge of the top square.

Getting started

Use the Cutting List on p. 11 as a guide for cutting all the parts. The next step is to mark the shelf positions on the shelf sides. It's important to keep track of the orientation of the parts. For reference, we placed a piece of masking tape on the top of each side, and on the top side of each shelf. Use a framing square to draw lines indicating the bottom of each shelf (Photo 1).

No need to mark the location of biscuits on the shelves and sides. Instead make marks on the scrap of wood used as a fence. Draw marks to indicate the outside edges of the 1x8 shelves and sides, and mark 1-3/4 in. in from each edge to indicate the center of the biscuits. To use the fence, line up the outside marks with the edges of the part you're cutting slots in. And then line up the center mark on the biscuit-joining tool with the marks for the center of the biscuits (Photos 3 and 4).

To mark the legs and sides for biscuits, set the legs in position and make pairs of marks that line up with each other on the legs and sides (Photo 2). Put a piece of masking tape on the top of each 2x2 leg, and keep this facing up when you cut the biscuit slots. Photo 7 shows how to bevel the legs.

Cut slots for the biscuits

Biscuit joiners have a flip-down fence that can be used to position the slots, but instead we're showing a method that allows you to reference the slots from

FRAMING SQUARE

LINE FOR BOTTOM OF SHELF

1 **Mark both sides at once.** Lay the bookcase sides together to mark the shelf locations. The layout marks have to be perfect, so closely supervise this step.

LEG

SIDE

MARKS FOR BISCUIT SLOTS

2 **Mark the biscuit slots.** Make pairs of corresponding marks on the legs and sides. Later you'll center the biscuit joiner on the marks to cut slots that align.

Four biscuit joiner techniques

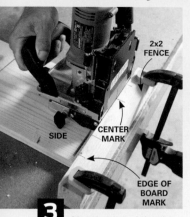

3 **Slot the end of the side.** Clamp the fence to the work surface and butt the end of the shelf to it. Then center the biscuit joiner on the mark and cut the slot. Repeat for the second slot.

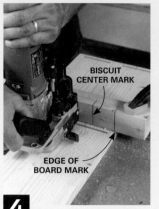

4 **Cut slots for the shelves.** Line up the 2x2 jig with the edge of board mark and clamp it. Center the biscuit joiner on the center mark on the fence and cut the slot. Repeat for the second slot.

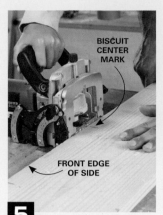

5 **Cut slots for the legs.** Line up the center of the biscuit joiner with the marks on the edge of the side and cut the slots. Make sure both the shelf side and the biscuit joiner are tight to the work surface when you cut the slot.

6 **Position the slot with a spacer.** Place a scrap of 1/2-in. plywood or particleboard on the work surface. Butt the leg against it and rest the biscuit joiner on the spacer while you cut the slots. The 1/2-in. spacer will automatically position the slots.

the base of the biscuit joiner. Photos 3 – 6 show the techniques. For a more detailed description of this method, go to familyhandyman.com and type "biscuit joints" into the search box.

Older kids and teens won't have any trouble mastering the biscuit joiner. With a little coaching, they'll be cutting slots like a pro. What's trickiest about cutting the slots is keeping track of the orientation of the parts. Just remember to keep the masking tape facing up, with one exception: The slots on the 1x8 top should be cut with the tape side down.

Glue the bookcase together

Here's where a helper really comes in handy. You have to work fast to spread the glue in the biscuit slots and onto the biscuits (Photo 8), and then assemble the parts before the glue starts to swell the biscuits (Photo 9).

Start by arranging all the parts on your work surface. Use a flux brush to spread the glue in the slots, and onto the biscuits after they are installed. Any small brush will work, though. When you have everything assembled, install clamps to hold the sides tight to the shelves while the glue dries. Check by using a framing square or by measuring diagonally from opposite corners to make sure the bookcase is square. Adjust it if needed. Then tighten the clamps. This is a good time to take a break while you let the glue dry for about an hour.

Build the top

To minimize potential cupping, we decided to make the top by gluing two pieces of 1x6 together rather than using a solid board. Choose a straight piece of 1x6 with a sharp, clean edge. Cut the pieces long and trim the top to length

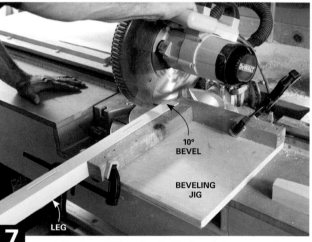

7 **Bevel the legs with a simple jig.** Screw two scraps to a small square of plywood to form a cradle for the legs. Clamp the jig to the miter saw fence, and cut a 10-degree bevel on the bottom of each leg.

8 **Add the biscuits.** Work quickly to glue biscuits into the slots. Spread the glue in the slots, and onto the biscuits, with a brush.

Materials List

ITEM	QTY.
1x8 x 8' No. 2 pine boards	2
1x6 x 8' No. 2 pine board	1
1x6 x 10' No. 2 pine board	1
2x4 x 8' pine (rip to 2x2s for legs)	1
No. 20 wood biscuits	39
1-1/2" wood screws	24
1-1/4" drywall or wood screws	4
1/4" flat washers	4
Bottle of wood glue	1

Cutting List

KEY	QTY.	SIZE & DESCRIPTION
A	2	3/4" x 7-1/4" x 36" pine sides
B	5	3/4" x 7-1/4" x 22-1/2" pine shelves, top and bottom
C	4	1-1/2" x 1-1/2" x 39" pine legs
D	2	3/4" x 5-1/2" x 28" pine top (trim to 26-1/2" after joining)
E	4	3/4" x 5-1/2" x 36" pine back

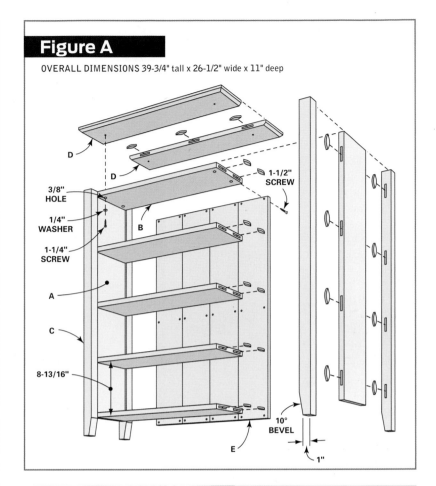

Figure A

OVERALL DIMENSIONS 39-3/4" tall x 26-1/2" wide x 11" deep

3/8" HOLE

1/4" WASHER

1-1/4" SCREW

1-1/2" SCREW

8-13/16"

10° BEVEL

1"

9 **Assemble the shelves quickly.** Biscuits start to swell and lock in place soon after the glue is applied, so it's important to get the shelves assembled quickly.

10 **Beveling the edge is a job for Dad.** Use a router and a 45-degree chamfering bit to bevel the front and sides of the top. Your helper can hold the top to keep it from shifting on the Bench Cookies.

BISCUIT

TOP   45° BEVEL

BENCH COOKIE

after you glue the two parts together. For pro tips on gluing boards edge-to-edge, go to familyhandyman.com and enter "edge gluing" in the search box. Cut biscuit slots in the sides of the two 1x6s to help hold them in alignment while installing the clamps. Glue and clamp the two 1x6s. Then let the glue set up about 30 minutes before routing the edge (Photo 10).

Add the legs, top and back

The legs are held to the sides of the bookcase with biscuits. When attached, the legs should protrude 1/2 in. past the outside, and overlap the shelves by 1/4 in. Glue in the biscuits, spread a line of glue along the edge of the side, and clamp the legs to the sides (Photo 11). Let the glue set for about 30 minutes.

Drill four 3/8-in. holes at the corners of the bookcase top. The holes are oversized to allow the top to expand and contract. Attach the top with four 1-1/4-in. screws and 1/4-in. washers.

Complete the bookcase by screwing the four 1x6s to the back of the unit (Photo 12). Drill 1/8-in. pilot holes for the screws to avoid splitting.

A little final sanding and the bookcase will be ready for finish. Wipe-on poly or oil finish are both good options.

1-1/4"
SCREW

LEG

BEVEL SIDE

11 **Insert the biscuits and clamp the legs.** Spread the glue and insert the biscuits. Then glue on the legs. Clamp them and wait for the glue to dry before moving on to install the top and back.

12 **Screw on the back boards.** Drill pilot holes to prevent splitting. Then screw the boards to the back of the bookcase. With a little coaching, young helpers will be driving screws like a pro.

Get the job done FASTER
Sliding compound miter saw

KOBALT

They're accurate and portable, with the capacity to cut wide boards and trim. That's why every carpenter has one of these big bad boys. These 10-in. saws fall into two classes: saws that tilt only to one side like the Kobalt saw, left (mostly $200 or less) and pro tools that tilt to both sides like the Makita, right ($450 and up).

MAKITA

Shoe shelves

6-3/4"
1-3/8" — 3-1/2"
3/4" HOLE
5/8"
5-1/8"

1 Clamp the 1x3 support to a piece of scrap wood as you drill the holes to prevent the wood from splintering.

Without constant vigilance, shoes tend to pile up into a mess next to entry doors. Untangle the mess with a simple, attractive shoe shelf that keeps everything from boots to slippers organized and off the floor.

Cut and drill the dowel supports (Photo 1), then screw them to 1x4s (Photo 2). Cut the 1x4s to fit your shoes and the available space—an average pair of adult shoes needs a 10-in.-wide space. Nail or glue the dowels into the dowel supports, leaving 2 in. (or more) extending beyond the supports at the end to hang sandals or slippers.

Apply finish before you mount the shoe shelves to the wall. Screw the shoe shelves to studs or use heavy-duty toggle-bolt style anchors to hold it in place.

WHAT IT TAKES

Time: 2 hours
Skill level: Beginner

5/8" DOWEL

45° CUT

2"

1-5/8" SCREWS

2 Predrill through the back of the 1x4 into the 1x3 supports, then glue and screw the pieces together.

Simple bin tower

Tons of easy-access storage—and more space to hang stuff!

WHAT IT TAKES

Time: 1 day
Skill level: Beginner

Stop digging through stacks of storage bins every time you need something. This bin storage system gives you quick and easy access to all your bins.

These bin towers are simple to build, don't require expensive tools, and actually add wall space without losing a lot of floor space. We designed the towers to fit 16- to 18-gallon bins with a lid size of about 18 x 24 in. You'll have so much extra space when you're done that you can go buy a few more tools!

1 **Fill plywood voids.** Figure out which edge will be exposed on each part, and fill any voids in the plywood. When the filler dries, sand the edge with 100-grit sandpaper.

Cut up the plywood

Use "BC" sanded pine plywood for this project. The holes and blemishes on the "B" side are filled and make for a good painting surface. It's not furniture grade, but it's priced right and works well for garage projects like this one. Rip all the sheets down to 23-3/4 in. If you don't own a table saw, use a straightedge and make your cuts with a circular saw.

Once all the sheets have been ripped down, cut the tops, bottoms and shelves to 18-in. lengths. If you're using a circular saw, save time by clamping two 8-ft. strips together, and cut two at a time. Some home centers will make your cuts for you, so if you don't have a ton of confidence in your cutting skills, ask the staff if they can help.

Paint the parts before assembly

Finishing the cut components before you assemble them will save you a bunch of time, but before you start slathering on the paint, figure out which edges need to be painted—the back edges of the sides don't, and only the front edges of the shelves do. Configure all the parts so the best edge faces out. Mark an "X" with a pencil on all the edges that needed paint. Some of the edges will have voids in the wood that will need to be filled (Photo 1).

Use a stainable wood filler if you plan to stain your project. Make a couple of passes with 100-grit sandpaper before you paint. Cover the wood with a paint/primer in one to save time (Photo 2). If you choose a traditional wood primer, have the store tint it close to the final color.

Assemble the towers

Use an 18-gauge brad nailer with 1-1/2-in. brads to quickly attach the shelves to the sides, three brads on each side. If you don't have a brad nailer, that's OK; you can assemble everything with screws only. Cut a piece of plywood 18-5/16 in. wide to align the shelves (Photo 3). The spacer board may scuff up the paint a little bit, but you can touch it up when you paint over your fastener holes after everything is all put together. Arrange the sides so the good surface faces out. The good surface on the bottom four shelves should face up, and the top two should face down. That way, you'll see the nicer finish from almost any angle.

2 **Finish before you assemble.** Save yourself a ton of time by painting or staining the individual components of this project before you assemble them.

Figure A

Bin tower

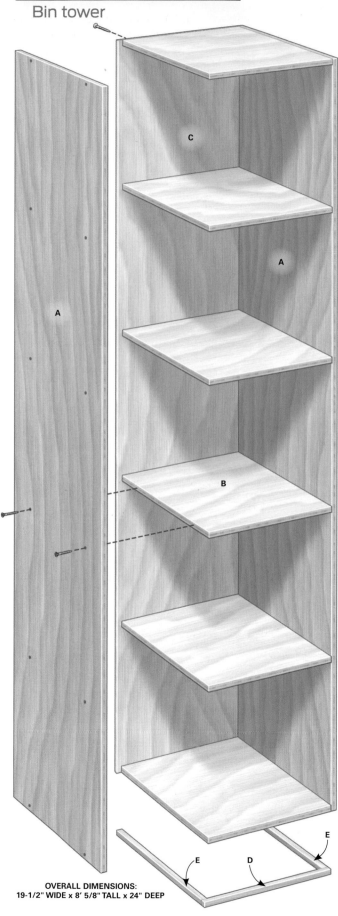

OVERALL DIMENSIONS:
19-1/2" WIDE x 8' 5/8" TALL x 24" DEEP

What it takes

(for three towers)

Cost: $250–$300 including paint and hardware

Skill: Beginner to intermediate

Tools: Table saw/circular saw, drill, 18-gauge brad nailer (optional)

Materials List

(for three towers)

ITEM	QTY.
4' x 8' x 3/4" BC sanded plywood	5
4' x 8' x 1/4" underlayment plywood	2
4' x 4' x 1/4" underlayment plywood	1
1x2 x 8' pressure-treated board	1
1" 18-gauge brads	
1-1/2" 18-gauge brads	
2" trim head screws	
Can of wood filler or patching compound	
Gallon of paint/primer	

Cutting List (for three towers)

KEY	QTY.	SIZE & DESCRIPTION
A	6	23-3/4" x 96" x 3/4" BC sanded pine plywood (sides)
B	18	18" x 23-3/4" x 3/4" BC sanded pine plywood (shelves)
C	3	19-1/2" x 96" x 1/4" sanded pine plywood (backs)
D	3	5/8" x 3/4" x 18-3/4" pressure-treated lumber (front bottom strip)
E	6	5/8" x 3/4" x 22-7/8" pressure-treated lumber (side bottom strip)

Figure B

Cutting diagrams for 3/4" plywood

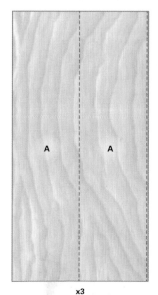

x3

x2

3 **Shoot, then screw.** Tack the shelves into position with a brad nailer. Then strengthen each connection with 2-in. trim head screws. A plywood spacer lets you position parts perfectly without measuring.

4 **Use the back as a square.** Use the factory-cut edges of the plywood back to square up your project. Start on the top or bottom, and then work your way up the side. Check for square before finishing it off. Reinforce it all with screws.

After everything is nailed together, come back and install two 2-in. trim head screws into each shelf (use three if you're not using brads). (Wood glue won't hold well because of the painted sides.)

Install the bottom strips

Plywood will eventually rot if it's sitting directly on a concrete floor. To avoid this, rip 5/8-in. strips from a 1x2 pressure-treated board and install them on the bottom (Photo 4). Four square blocks would also keep the plywood off the floor, but it creates a space where screws, washers or other little objects could get lost. Inset the strips about 3/8 in. and nail them on with 1-1/2-in. brads.

Fasten the back

Use the 1/4-in. plywood to square up the unit (Photo 4). Fasten the two factory-cut edges of the plywood to the back first using 1-in. brads. Nail the short side, and then the long side, aligning the edges as you go. Don't install a whole bunch of brads until you know everything is square. Flip the piece over and check for square using a framing square or by measuring from inside corner to inside corner on a couple of different openings—if the measurements are the same, you should be good to go. Finish fastening the back with brads spaced every 8 in. or so, then reinforce it with one 2-in. trim head screw in the center of each shelf and five screws on each side.

Screw it to the wall

In many garages, the concrete floor slopes toward the overhead door. That means you'll probably have to shim the bottom to get the bin tower to sit straight and tight up against the wall. We're big fans of composite shims: They don't compress as much as wood, they break off cleanly, and they won't ever rot. Set the first tower against the wall and shim the front until it sits tight against the wall. Use a level to check for plumb while you shim the low side. Insert at least four shims on the side and three on the front. Go back and snug up the front shims.

Once the tower is plumb, screw it to the wall studs with 2-in. screws. Make sure each tower is fastened to at least one stud. Since tipping is a concern, install a few screws near the top; you'll only need screws down low if you need to draw the tower tight to the wall.

Mark all the shims, and pull them out one at a time. Cut them down to size and replace them. Run a small bead of clear silicone around the bottom to hold the shims in place. If the towers ever get moved, the silicone will be easy to scrape off the floor. Finally, go get all sorts of caddies, hooks and hangers, and start organizing.

Suspended shelf

Steel cable and shaft collars add style & strength

This wall-hung bookshelf is one of the easiest we've ever built. If you can stack blocks, you can build it. And installing the cable doesn't require any more skill than drilling a hole. Things will go a lot quicker if you own a table saw, a miter saw and a pneumatic nailer, but you could easily build this project with just basic hand tools and a circular saw. We used a router to bevel the shelf edges, but this is optional.

If you use a penetrating oil finish, you can complete this in a day. For a urethane or painted finish, allow a few extra days—you'll need to prefinish the parts before assembly.

Cut the parts

Start by ripping the shelves to the widths given in the Cutting List (p. 21). We used a full-width 1x10 for the bottom shelf and successively narrower boards as we went up. Making all the shelves the same width would be OK, too. While you're at it,

WHAT IT TAKES

Time: 1 day
Skill level: Beginner

It's stronger than it looks

Your first question when you see this bookcase might be "Is it strong enough?" And the answer is a resounding yes. It's extra strong, in fact. The back edges of the shelves are securely supported with screws and blocks, and the front edges are hung from aircraft-strength cable. We even epoxied the top of the cable to the standards just to make sure. Each shelf is held up by shaft collars that are tightened onto the cables with set-screws. So don't worry about the strength. These shelves could hold your dumbbell collection!

1 **Drill an angled hole for the cable.** Start by drilling straight down about 1/8 in. Then tilt the drill to about a 45-degree angle and use the starter hole to keep the bit in place as you start to drill. The angle of the hole isn't critical.

TOP CLEAT
CABLE HOLE

2 **Nail the shelves to the cleats.** Drive a brad through the shelf into the support cleat. These brads just hold the shelves in place when you flip the bookshelf over to drive in the shelf screws (Photo 5) and secure the cable (Photo 6).

ALIGNMENT MARK
SHELF SCREW HOLE
TOP SHELF

3 **Assemble the shelves.** Add a cleat under the shelf and nail it in. Then add another shelf and tack it to the cleat. Continue like this until you get to the bottom. Now do the same thing on the other side.

CLEAT

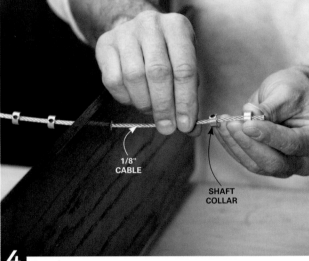

4 **Thread the cable.** Start at the bottom shelf and run the cable through the collars and shelves. Add two collars between each pair of shelves. At the top, thread the cable through the angled hole.

1/8" CABLE
SHAFT COLLAR

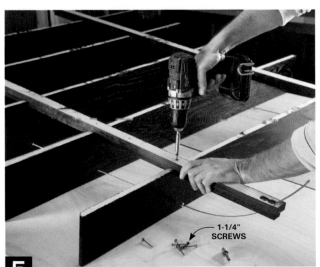

5 **Fasten the shelves.** Flip the bookshelf over and drive screws into the back of each shelf through the holes in the standards.

1-1/4" SCREWS

rip two 1-in.-wide strips from the 1x2s for the support cleats. Next, cut the boards to length. We used a 45-degree chamfer bit and router to bevel the ends and front edges of the shelves, but you could leave them square if you'd like. After the parts are cut and prefinished, you're ready to assemble the shelf.

Assemble the shelves

The shelves are too big to build on a normal workbench. If you're young and nimble, you could put them together on the floor. Otherwise, save your back and line up a few old doors on a pair of sawhorses.

Assembly is straightforward; follow Photos 1 – 6 and the details shown in Figures A and B. Here are a few tips to help:

■ Mark the back of the shelves 13 in. from the ends so you'll know where to line them up with the standards (Photo 2).

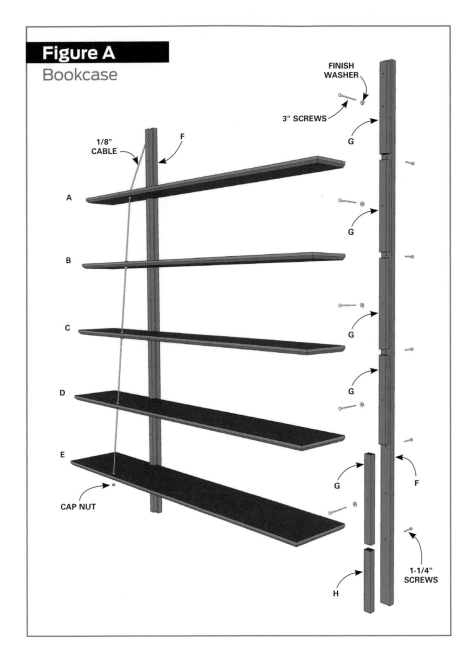

Figure A
Bookcase

FINISH WASHER

3" SCREWS

1/8" CABLE

F

G

G

G

G

A

B

C

D

E

CAP NUT

G

G

F

H

1-1/4" SCREWS

Materials List

ITEM	QTY.
1x10 x 5' board	2
1x8 x 5' board	2
1x6 x 5' board	1
1x2 x 6' board	4
1-1/4" wood screws	10
3" wood screws	10
No. 10 finish washers	10
3/8" steel washers	2
3/4" wood screws	2
Five-minute epoxy	1
No. 10-32 cap nuts	2

Cable and collars are available from McMaster-Carr (mcmaster.com). Enter the product numbers into the search box to find the items listed. You may also be able to find cable at home centers or hardware stores. The cable costs 62¢ per ft., and the collars are 89¢ each.

5/32" bore shaft collars (6432K73)	22
1/8" 6x7 fiber-core cable (3449T16)	14'

Cutting List

KEY	QTY.	SIZE & DESCRIPTION
A	1	3/4" x 5-1/4" x 59-1/2" shelf
B	1	3/4" x 6-1/4" x 59-1/2" shelf
C	1	3/4" x 7-1/4" x 59-1/2" shelf
D	1	3/4" x 8-1/4" x 59-1/2" shelf
E	1	3/4" x 9-1/4" x 59-1/2" shelf
F	2	3/4" x 1-1/2" x 68-1/4" standards
G	10	3/4" x 1" x 11-1/4" cleats
H	2	3/4" x 1" x 7-3/4" cleats

- Keep the shelves and standards at a right angle to each other as you attach the cleats. That'll ensure that the cleats fit tight to the shelves.
- Don't drive nails where you'll be drilling holes.
- Drill mounting screw holes after you have all the cleats installed. It's easier to do it before you mount the shelves on the wall.

String the cable

The cable is flexible and easy to cut, so it's a breeze to install. Just remember to put two collars on the cable, between each pair of shelves, as you thread the cable through the holes. Leave about 4 in. of cable sticking out the top and an extra foot or so on the bottom. The extra cable on the bottom lets you use our "cable pedal" method for removing slack (Photo 8). After stringing the cable, flip the whole works over so you can drive the shelf screws (Photo 5) and anchor the top of the cable

(Photo 6). Take a coffee break while the epoxy sets up.

Mount the shelves

The shelf standards are spaced 32 in. on center to align with studs. So all you have to do is locate two studs where you want the shelves to go and mark them with masking tape. Setting the shelves on blocks (Photo 7) is a handy way to hold them up while you drive the first few screws. Start by driving one of the top screws. Before you drive the top screw in the second standard, check to make sure the shelves are level. After the two top screws are in place, make sure the standards are plumb before you drive the remaining screws. We used No. 10 finish washers under the screws for a decorative effect.

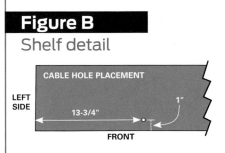

Figure B
Shelf detail

CABLE HOLE PLACEMENT

LEFT SIDE

13-3/4"

1"

FRONT

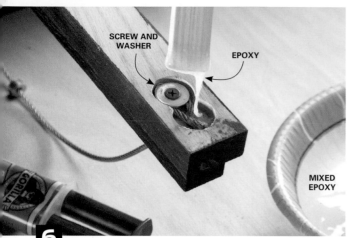

6 **Anchor the cable with epoxy.** Loop the cable in the recess and hold it down with a washer and screw. Then mix five-minute epoxy and fill the recess with it.

7 **Mount the bookshelf.** Locate two studs that are 32 in. apart with a stud finder. Screw the standards to the studs, making sure the shelves are level and the standards are plumb.

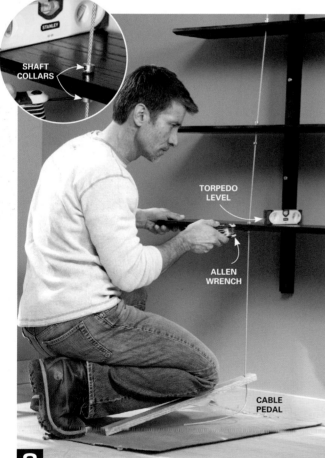

8 **Tension the cables.** Tighten the cable using a scrap of wood with a hole in it to put tension on the cable while you tighten the setscrew on the collar below the lowest shelf. Then snug the remaining collars to the top and bottom of the shelves and tighten the collars.

9 **Trim and cap the cable.** Use a side-cutting pliers or lineman's pliers to cut the cable. Leave 1/4 in. protruding. Cover the end of the cable with a cap nut. Use hot-melt glue or silicone caulk to hold the cap nut in place.

Tighten the cable

At this point, the cable is slack and the collars are still loose. Your goal is to take the slack out of the cable and then adjust each shelf so it's level from front to back while you tighten the collars (Photo 8). Use an Allen wrench to tighten the setscrews. Remember, you don't need too much tension on the cable, just enough to remove the slack. Finish up by cutting the cable and covering the end with a cap nut (Photo 9).

Regrout a shower

By itself, the tile in a shower enclosure is almost maintenance free. With an occasional wipe-down, it can look good for years. Grout, however, is a different story—eventually it's going to break down. Large cracks and crumbly chunks are alarming, but smaller fractures can be trouble too. Fractures, and stains that won't wash out, may indicate spots where water is leaking in and working its way behind the tiles. Sooner or later, that water will weaken the adhesive that's holding the tile or cause rot in the walls. When that happens, the only solution is to tear out the tile and start from scratch.

The good news is that if you catch it in time, you can quickly and easily give tiled surfaces a new lease on life—and a fresh look—by applying a new layer of grout. The following pages walk you through the regrouting process from start to finish and offer tools and tips to prevent mid-job mishaps. You don't need previous tile experience; regrouting is mostly grunt work.

The materials needed for an average-size shower cost about $50. In some cases, you can finish the job in a few hours, but to be safe, give yourself a day or two. If you start on Saturday morning, you should be able to take a shower on Monday.

Choosing the right tools and grout

Before you begin digging into that old grout, make sure you have all the tools and materials you'll need to finish the job. Think of this project in three parts: scraping and cleaning, regrouting and cleanup.

When you're choosing grout-removal tools, stick with steel to be safe. Many special grout scrapers equipped with carbide tips work well and stay sharp for a long time, but if you slip, the carbide can damage your tile or tub. Steel utility knife blades, on the other hand, may dull quickly, but they're less likely to scratch the tile. Buy a knife with easy-to-change blades, and also buy plenty of spare blades (a 100-blade pack only costs about $10). They're ideal for cleaning out narrow joints. A manual grout saw (Photo 2) with a notched steel blade is also handy for stubborn chunks of grout.

When the going gets tough

The basic arsenal of simple scratch-out tools works for most projects, but there are times when you might need a little extra help. This pair of not-so-secret weapons can make short work of super-stubborn grout and caulk.

The first is a grout saw attachment. Attached to a reciprocating saw or oscillating tool (there are different types), this carbide-tipped clean-out tool works like a steroid-fueled electric toothbrush. Controlling the blade so it doesn't scratch the tile may take some getting used to, so start with light pressure. Once the blade digs in, it's not too difficult to keep it on the path.

The second weapon is caulk remover. You'll find it indispensable if the previous installers used silicone caulk to seal cracks around tubs and showers. Silicone's stickiness can make removing it a real headache. The chemical requires a few hours to soften stubborn caulk, but waiting is better than the tedious chore of scratching off the silicone remnants with your knife and possibly damaging your tile or tub.

GROUT SAW **CAULK REMOVER**

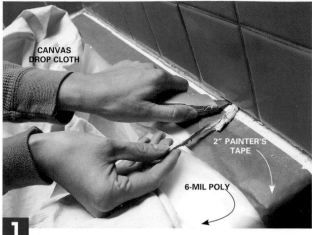

1 Slice along each edge of the caulk/wall joint with a sharp utility knife. Pull out the old caulk.

CANVAS DROP CLOTH
2" PAINTER'S TAPE
6-MIL POLY

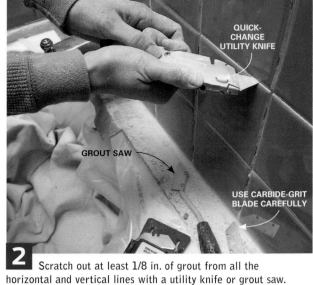

2 Scratch out at least 1/8 in. of grout from all the horizontal and vertical lines with a utility knife or grout saw. Change blades often.

QUICK-CHANGE UTILITY KNIFE
GROUT SAW
USE CARBIDE-GRIT BLADE CAREFULLY

3 Clean out all of the dust and loose debris from the grout joints using a stiff brush and vacuum.

STIFF BRUSH

As for grout, buy a 10-lb. bag—you may have some left over, but that's better than running out. Grout comes in two forms: unsanded and sanded. Your choice depends on the width of the gaps between the tiles. For joints up to 1/8 in., choose the unsanded variety. For wider joints, choose sanded to avoid cracking. Whatever type you need, look for a "polymer-modified" mix. The extra ingredients help prevent future cracking and staining. It's almost impossible to match new grout to old, but don't worry. By scratching out the topmost layer from all the grout lines and adding new, you'll get a fresh, consistent color.

To apply the grout, buy a rubber-soled grout float and a grout sponge. In case the grout starts hardening too quickly, you'll also want to buy a plastic scouring pad. Last, buy a tube of tub-and-tile caulk that matches the grout color.

Slice out caulk and scratch out grout

Before you begin your attack, take a minute to protect your tub against scratches and debris that can clog your drain (Photo 1). Tape a layer of plastic sheeting to your tub's top edge. Next, lay a drop cloth on top of the plastic to protect the tub and cushion your knees. Then remove the faucet hardware or protect it with masking tape.

HOLDS PEAKS
DRILL SET ON "SLOW"
POLYMER-MODIFIED GROUT
PAINT-MIXING PADDLE

4 Mix the grout with water in a tall bucket using a paint-mixing paddle. Mix slowly until the grout becomes a thick paste.

tip When you're shopping for grout, stick with brands that offer color-matching caulks. Factory-matched caulk/grout combinations blend almost perfectly.

5 Spread grout at an angle to the grout lines with a rubber float. Press hard on the float to pack the joints full of grout.

6 Scrape off excess grout by tipping the float on edge and pushing it diagonally across the tile. Work quickly.

Getting rid of the old caulk and grout requires plenty of elbow grease, but it's not difficult work, especially if you take your time. Begin by cutting out the old caulk (Photo 1) and then move on to the grout (Photo 2). When you're using a utility knife, switch blades as soon as the edge stops digging and starts skating on the grout (Photo 2). At times, you may have more success with the grout saw. Whatever tool you choose, the goal remains the same: to remove about 1/8 in. from the top (or more, if the grout comes out easily).

When you're done, remove dust and debris, which can weaken the bond between the tile and the new grout (Photo 3).

Mix the grout and pack the joints

Once the grout is mixed, the clock starts ticking toward the moment when it will harden on the wall…or in the bucket. Pro tilers can mix and use a 10-lb. bag of grout before it hardens, but to play it safe, mix up a few cups at a time and work in sections. A smaller batch will allow you plenty of time to apply it and clean the excess from one wall at a time. When you run out, rinse the container before mixing a new batch.

Before you make a batch from a bag, shake the bag to redistribute any pigment and Portland cement that might have settled out in shipment. After it's been dry mixed, scoop out a few cups (one cup equals about a half pound) into a bucket. The instructions on the bag indicate how much water to add per pound of mix. To ensure a strong mix, start with about three-quarters of the specified amount of water and gradually pour in just enough to make the grout spreadable. Aim for a fairly stiff consistency, somewhere between cake icing and peanut butter (Photo 4, inset). Don't worry if the grout looks a little lumpy. After it's mixed, allow it to sit for 10 minutes. During this time, the remaining dry specks will absorb moisture. Give the grout one last stir (restirring also keeps the mix from hardening in your bucket) and it's ready for application.

Focus on one wall at a time. Scoop out some grout with a rubber float and press it out across the tiles at a 45-degree angle (Photo 5). It's OK to be messy. The goal is to pack as much grout into the joints as you can. Press hard and

7 Wipe off the excess grout with a damp sponge as soon as the grout lines are firm. To keep the rinse water clean, dip the sponge in the "dirty" bucket and wring it out. Then dip it in the "clean" bucket and wring it over the dirty bucket.

work the float in several directions.

Immediately after you fill the joints, rake off the excess grout and put it back in your bucket. Hold the float on edge, and remove the excess (Photo 6). Move the float across the joints diagonally to prevent the edge from dipping into the joints and pulling out too much grout. Work quickly before the grout starts to harden.

The time between scraping and sponging varies from job to job. Depending on your mix, the humidity or the temperature, the grout may take anywhere from five to 20 minutes to firm up. Begin sponging as soon as the grout feels firm and no longer sticks to your finger.

Using a well-wrung tile sponge, wipe away the bulk

8 Scrape grout out of the inside corners and tub/tile joint so that you can seal these joints with caulk later on.

9 Buff the haze off the tile after the grout dries (several hours). Use an old terry cloth towel.

HAZE

of the unwanted grout with short, gentle, circular strokes (Photo 7). Turn the sponge so that you're using a clean edge with each pass. Rinse and wring it out in the "dirty" bucket, then dip the sponge in a "clean" bucket, and finally wring it out again in the "dirty" bucket. This two-bucket technique helps keep your sponge and rinse water clean so that you can remove grout more effectively. Wring out as much water as possible. Too much water can pull cement and pigment from your fresh grout lines.

In addition to wiping away the excess, the sponge works for fine-tuning the shape of your grout lines. To shave down any high spots and make the lines slightly convex, run the sponge across the joint until the grout lines appear uniform. (If you find a low spot, use your finger to rub in a little extra grout.)

Finally, scrape out any globs of grout that may have gotten into the joints you intend to caulk (Photo 8). This includes all corners and the tub/tile joint. You could do this chore later, but it's a lot easier now, before the grout is rock hard.

The sponge-wiped walls may look clean at first, but as the surface moisture evaporates, the remaining grout particles will create a light haze. Give the grout an hour or two to dry, then buff off any residual haze with a soft towel (Photo 9).

Finish up with neat caulk joints

Let the grout dry overnight before applying the caulk along the tub/tile joint and inside corners. For clean, precise caulk lines, run painter's tape along the inside corner and at the tub/tile joint (Photo 10). Just remember to remove the tape as soon as you finish smoothing. If you wait too long, the caulk will skin over or stick to the tape and you'll pull out the caulk when you try to remove the tape. Depending on the caulk, your bath should be ready in 24 hours.

To reduce mold growth, seal grout lines for extra stain and water resistance. Give the grout a week or two to cure completely before sealing. Remember that sealers wear off over time, so you'll need to reapply it every year or so. If you don't want to apply a sealer, wiping your walls down with a squeegee after each shower works almost as well.

COLOR-MATCHING CAULK

3/16" GAP

DRIPLESS CAULK GUN

10 Apply painter's tape to control your caulk lines. Apply the caulk, smooth the joint with your finger and immediately remove the tape.

tip The biggest mistake you're likely to make is waiting too long before sponging the excess grout off the tile.

A plastic scrub pad is a cheap insurance policy. The coarse pad quickly and easily scours off hardened grout that a sponge won't pick up, but it won't scratch the tile.

Of course, buying one may guarantee that you won't need it. On the other hand, should you need one, you won't be able to drive to the hardware store fast enough.

Hide valuables
in your kitchen

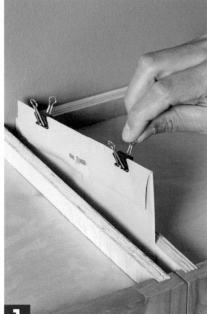

1 **Cabinet hidey-hole.** Between almost every pair of upper cabinets, there's a 1/2-in. gap. Take advantage of that gap by hanging a manila envelope containing, oh, about two grand in hundred-dollar bills? Hang the cash with binder clips that are too wide to fall through the crack.

2 **False-bottom drawer.** Pick a deep drawer so the depth change won't be obvious. Cut 1/4-in. plywood 1/16 in. smaller than the drawer opening and rest it on a couple of wood strips that are hot-glued to the drawer sides. Then hot-glue some item you'd expect to find in that drawer to the bottom so you have a handle to lift the false bottom and reveal the booty.

3 **Toe-kick hideaway.** There's an enormous 4-in.-tall cavity under all those kitchen cabinets behind the toe-kicks. It takes a few carpentry skills, but you can pull the toe-kicks free and make them removable. Most are 1/4-in. plywood held in place with 1-in. brads, and they're pretty easy to pull off. If you have a secondary 3/4-in. toe-kick, you'll have to cut it out at both ends. An oscillating tool works well for that task. Stick both halves of round hook-and-loop self-adhesive tape to the toe-kick. Then push the toe-kick into place. The adhesive will stick to the cabinet base and leave half of the hook-and-loop tape in place when you pull it free. You can store approximately $2.4 million in gold bullion under two average-size cabinets—provided the floor is strong enough to support it.

4 **Counterfeit containers.** Go online and type in "secret hiding places" and you'll be amazed by how many brand-name phony containers are available. Comet, Coca-Cola, Bush Beans—whatever. But you can craft a homemade version too. This mayonnaise jar had its interior spray-painted with cream-colored paint for plastic.

5 **The appliance caper.** Fridges and dishwashers have a snap-off grille in the front. Well, there's a lot of secret storage space under there. Ask yourself this: How many burglars will be thinking about cleaning your refrigerator coils? But before you stuff treasures under a fridge, take a peek to see where the coils are. On some models, a stack of cash might block the airflow. That will make the fridge work harder and could even damage it.

Glass panels for cabinet doors

A pair of glass doors can add a designer touch to any kitchen. They can turn an ordinary cabinet into a decorative showcase or simply break up an otherwise monotonous row of solid doors. This alteration works only for frame-and-panel cabinet doors (see Figure A), where you can replace the inset wood panels with glass. Converting the two doors shown here took about two hours.

To get started, remove the doors from the cabinets and remove all hardware from the doors. Examine the back side of each door; you might find a few tiny nails where the panel meets the frame. If so, gouge away wood with a utility knife to expose the nail heads and pull the nails with a pliers. Look carefully; just one leftover nail will chip your expensive router bit.

Cut away the lips using a router and a 1/2-in. pattern bit (Photo 1). A pattern bit is simply a straight bit equipped with a bearing that rolls along a guide. Some home centers and hardware stores carry pattern bits, or you can search online for "pattern bits." Be sure to choose a bit that has the bearing on the top, not at the bottom.

Use any straight, smooth material (solid wood, plywood or MDF) to make two 3-1/2-in.-wide guides. To allow for the 1-in. cutting depth of our pattern bit, we nailed layers of plywood and MDF together to make 1-3/8-in.-thick guides. Position the guides 1/2 in. from the inner edges of the lips and clamp them firmly in place over the door. Support the outer edges of the guides with strips of wood that match the thickness of the door to keep them level (Photo 1). Before you start routing, make sure the door itself is clamped firmly in place.

Set the router on the guide and adjust the cutting depth so that the bit just touches the panel. Cut away the lips on two sides, then reposition the guides to cut away the other two. With the lips removed, lift the panel out

WHAT IT TAKES

Time: 2 hours
Skill level: Intermediate

STILE

PANEL

RAIL

LIP

Figure A
Panel door profile

Most cabinet doors are made like this one: A raised or flat panel fits into grooves in the rails-and-stile frame. To remove the panel, just cut away the lips on the back side of the door.

GUIDE

LIP

SUPPORT
STRIP

BEARING

PATTERN BIT

1 Clamp router guides to the back side of the door. Run a pattern bit along the guides to cut away the inside lips.

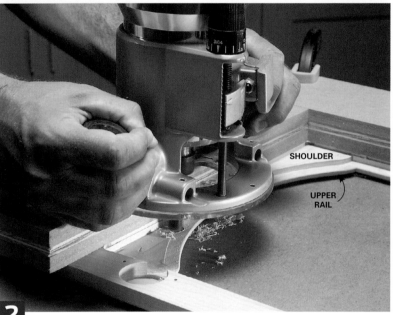

SHOULDER

UPPER
RAIL

2 Lower the router bit and cut away the shoulders on the back side of an arched upper rail to create a square recess for the glass.

GLASS
CLIP

3 Set the glass into the frame and secure it with glass clips placed no more than 12 in. apart. Then reinstall the doors.

of the frame. If the panel is stuck, a few light hammer taps will free it.

If your door frame has a rectangular opening, it's now ready for glass. If it has an arched upper rail, cut a square recess above the arch (Photo 2). This allows you to use a rectangular piece of glass rather than a curved piece (curved cuts are expensive). Then simply lay the glass in and anchor it with glass clips (Photo 3). Clips are available from the glass supplier or online (search for "glass door retainer clips").

GLASS
CLIPS

If the glass rattles in the frame, add pea-size blobs of hot-melt glue every 12 in.

Buying glass

Most hardware stores carry clear glass and will cut it for free or a small fee. Ask for 3/16-in.-thick "double strength" glass. Order glass panels 1/8 in. smaller than the recess in the frame. To find tempered, textured or colored glass ($5 to $15 per sq. ft.), do a search online for "glass." We bought clear textured glass and paid the supplier an extra $60 to have the two panels tempered. Building codes require tempered glass for locations within 5 ft. of the floor.

Metal panels for cabinet doors

WHAT IT TAKES

Time: 2 hours
Skill level: Intermediate

PANEL

LIP

1 A door panel fits into grooves in the door's frame. To remove a panel, just cut away the lips on the back of the door.

Installing new panels in old cabinet doors can really dress up a kitchen (and new panels are *a lot* cheaper than new cabinets). Insert materials include glass, translucent plastic, copper, metal, fabric, wicker and many others. Adding "feature" inserts to just one or two of your cabinet doors can be striking and very inexpensive.

Remove the panels

To cut away the lips that secure the door panel (Photo 1), you'll need a pattern bit—a straight router bit with a bearing that's the same diameter as the cutting diameter (see photos, p. 31). You can buy a pattern bit for about $25, but most are too long to use with a 3/4-in.-thick guide. You may have to shop online to find a shorter bit with a cutting depth of 1/2 in.

If you're working with just one or two cabinet doors, the only guide you'll need is a straight board. If you have a stack of doors to rout, a more elaborate guide will save you time (Photo 2). The stops automatically position the guide without measuring, and you can rout two sides without repositioning.

Examine the back of the door before you rout. If you find any nails, pull them out so they don't chip your router bit. Before you start cutting, set your router depth

2 Run a pattern bit along a guide to remove the lips. Any straight board will work as a guide, but an L-shaped guide with stops speeds up the job.

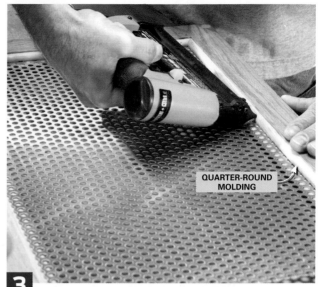

3 Frame the back of the insert with quarter-round molding to hold the metal in place. If you use a nail gun, aim carefully so you don't shoot through the face of the door.

so the bit just touches the panel. After you cut away the lips, simply lift out the door panel. The router bit will leave rounded corners at each corner of the door frame; square them off with a chisel or utility knife.

Install the metal inserts

Prefinish 1/4-in. quarter-round molding and use it to secure the inserts (Photo 3). When you place the insert into the door frame, make sure the punched side is face up (the punched side will feel slightly raised around the holes). Fasten the quarter-round with 5/8-in. nails or brads. If you don't have a brad nailer or pinner, you can use a hammer; just be careful not to dent the metal.

Buying metal inserts

Some home centers carry sheets of metal (including perforated) and will cut them for you for a small fee. But you'll find a much bigger selection online. Look for metal in the 16- to 20-gauge range. The metal inserts shown here were purchased from an online dealer and were ordered over the phone.

Do your measuring after you remove the cabinet doors to get accurate insert measurements. Order inserts 1/8 in. shorter in both the length and the width so the inserts just fit in the opening. If stainless is out of your price range, consider aluminum or plain steel (called "mill finish"). You can spray-paint your metal any color you want. No matter what finish you order, wash the metal with paint thinner to rinse off the manufacturing oils. If you choose not to paint the steel, spray it with a clear lacquer to prevent it from rusting

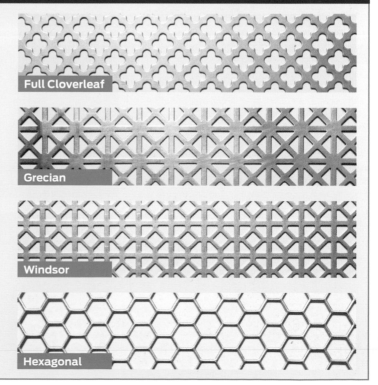

Full Cloverleaf

Grecian

Windsor

Hexagonal

Install a faucet

Today's faucets are easier than ever to install. In fact, you can even buy faucets that install entirely from the top of the sink so you don't have to crawl underneath. But there are still things you should know for a quick, easy and leak-free installation. Here are our best tips for helping you with your next faucet installation.

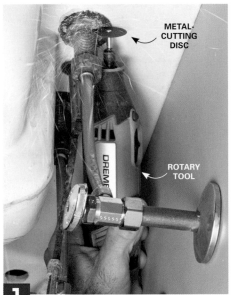

METAL-CUTTING DISC

DREMEL

ROTARY TOOL

1 **Cut out the old faucet.** Even with a basin wrench, it can be nearly impossible to break loose corroded nuts holding older faucets to the sink. If you don't care about wrecking the faucet, cut off the nuts instead. You can use either a rotary tool with a grinding disc or an oscillating tool with a metal-cutting blade. Cut through one side of the nut. Then use a screwdriver to pry the nut away from the faucet body. You can also cut off other stubborn parts, like the pop-up drain assembly on a bathroom sink.

WHAT IT TAKES **Time:** 3 hours
Skill level: Beginner

2 **Check for leaks.** When you're done with the faucet installation, check for leaks. Turn on the water and let it run for two or three minutes. Then crawl under the sink with some tissue and wipe around the joints with it. Even a tiny leak will show up as a wet spot on the tissue. Tighten the connection near any leak you find.

CLEAR SILICONE CAULK

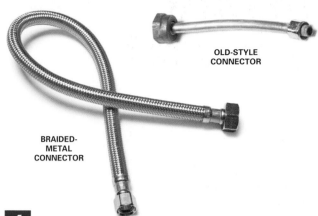

OLD-STYLE CONNECTOR

BRAIDED-METAL CONNECTOR

3 **Mount the faucet with silicone.** If water gets under your faucet, it can corrode the faucet or worse, damage your countertop or cabinet. Most new faucets include a gasket of some type to create a seal between the faucet and the sink, but it's still a good idea to apply a bead of clear silicone caulk to the bottom of the faucet and the bottom of the gasket to ensure a good seal. Also, the silicone acts as an adhesive to prevent the faucet from moving around if the connection nuts loosen. Clean up any silicone that oozes out, first using just a paper towel, then mineral spirits.

4 **Upgrade your supply lines.** One of the most difficult parts of installing a new faucet used to be connecting the supply lines so they didn't leak. But the new-style connectors with braided jackets have gaskets built into each end that make connections virtually foolproof. They cost more but are worth every penny. You don't need to crank the nut very tight for an effective seal. Just thread it finger-tight and then add about a half-turn with a wrench. So save yourself headaches and replace those old supply lines with braided stainless steel connectors.

SHUTOFF VALVE

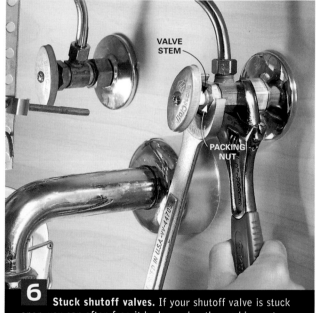

VALVE STEM

PACKING NUT

6 **Stuck shutoff valves.** If your shutoff valve is stuck open, you can often free it by loosening the packing nut slightly. This relieves pressure on the valve stem and allows you to turn the valve more easily. Retighten the valve stem nut just enough to prevent leaks around the valve stem.

5 **Measure for the supply lines.** Many new faucets include supply lines, but they may not be long enough, or they may not have the right threads to connect to your shutoff valves. To determine the length of the supply lines you'll need, measure from the underside of the sink near where the faucet connects to the shutoff valve and add a few inches. If the supply lines included with your new faucet aren't long enough, buy extensions. To make sure the threads on your new supply lines match those on your shutoff valves, take one of your old supply lines with you to the store and match it with the new supply lines.

7 **Remove the aerator before you turn on the water.** Messing around with plumbing often dislodges minerals or other debris that has built up inside the pipes and valves. To prevent that stuff from clogging the aerator in your new faucet, remove the aerator before turning the water back on. The aerator is the device on the end of your faucet that has a screen or perforated plastic covering the end. Most aerators simply unscrew counterclockwise. Some new faucets include a special tool for removing the aerator.

If you're installing a pullout faucet, the aerator can be tricky to remove. If this is the case, simply unscrew the entire spray head from the supply tube and point the tube into the sink while you turn on the water. Let the water run a few seconds. Then replace the aerator or spray head. If your faucet ever starts to run slowly, remove the aerator and clean it. This will usually fix the problem.

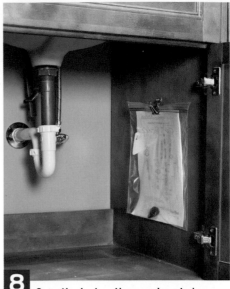

8 **Save the instructions and parts in a freezer bag.** Many new faucets include wrenches, aerator removal tools, and other parts or tools that you should keep. An easy way to keep track of this stuff, along with the instruction sheet, is to put it all in a big freezer bag and hang it inside the sink cabinet, where you'll always be able to find it.

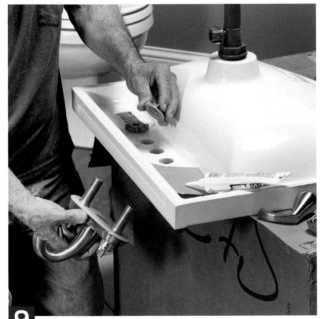

9 **Premount the faucet on new sink installations.** If you're installing a new sink along with your faucet, mount the faucet to the sink before you install the sink. It's much simpler than lying on your back inside the sink cabinet to install the faucet. Even if you're not installing a new sink, you may find it easier to remove the old sink to get better access for removing the old faucet and installing the new one. Plus, removing and reinstalling the old sink will allow you to clean off old caulk and gunk that's accumulated around the edge and renew the seal between the counter and the sink with fresh caulk.

10 **You may need a basin wrench.** A basin wrench is a standard plumbing tool that is indispensable for removing and installing most faucets. The wrench allows you to reach into the cramped area behind the sink to loosen or tighten the nuts that hold the faucet to the sink, and the nuts that connect the supply lines. You may not need a basin wrench if you can get the old faucet out by cutting the nuts (see Step 1) and if the new faucet includes a wrench or some other means of installing the faucet without a basin wrench. Check inside the package when you buy the faucet to see what's required. If you do need a basin wrench, plan to spend about $20 to get a good one.

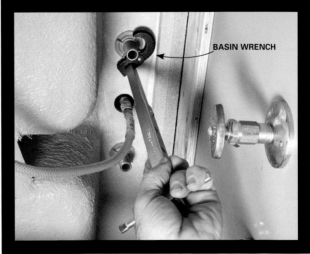

Reverse-osmosis water filter system

WHAT IT TAKES **Time:** 2 hours **Skill level:** Beginner

If you buy lots of bottled or filtered water or you're worried about your tap water, a reverse-osmosis water filter can be a good investment. For $150 to $300, it can provide 10 or more gallons of drinking water a day. Replacement filters will cost $100 to $200 annually.

Reverse-osmosis filters remove many pollutants and chemicals, separating them from the water and then flushing them into the drain line. The purified water is then fed to the storage tank or the spout on the sink. However, reverse-osmosis filters remove the minerals like calcium and magnesium that give water its taste, so try a gallon (available at most supermarkets) before buying a system.

First, hang the filter assembly on the back or side wall of the sink base (or in the basement close to the sink location) at the height specified in the instructions. Turn off both the cold and the hot water shutoffs, and then install (after the cold water shutoff) the tee or saddle valve included with the unit.

Cut the color-coded water supply line so that it's above the cabinet base and won't get kinked. Fasten the plastic tubing to the supply valve (Photo 1).

Shorten the supply and waste lines to the faucet to eliminate excess tubing, but don't cut the larger black waste line yet. Attach the lines to the fittings on the base of the faucet (Photo 2). The black waste lines feed through the base of the faucet to keep them above possible sink backups, but they have no connection to the supply.

Fasten the faucet to the sink, then install the drain-line adapter under the sink basket. Cut the waste line so that it flows downhill with no loops, then push it into the adapter (Photo 3).

Set the storage tank into place and install the final water line. Sterilize and fill the system according to the manufacturer's instructions (Photo 4).

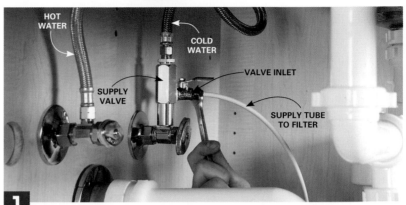

1 Push the plastic supply tube onto the supply valve, then tighten the nut a half turn past hand-tight.

2 Feed the water supply line and the two waste lines up through the hole in the sink and through the gasket and faucet base, then attach them.

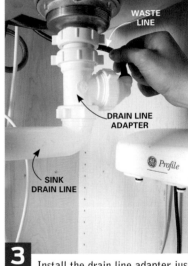

3 Install the drain line adapter just below the sink and above the discharge from the disposer and/or dishwasher.

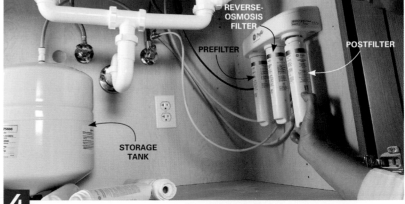

4 Push the plastic supply tube onto the supply valve, then tighten the nut a half turn past hand-tight.

Choose a faucet you'll love

Most people choose a faucet based on looks alone. And that's a mistake. Looks are important, but you can usually get the look you want without compromising on convenience and long-term dependability. For advice on those practical considerations, we talked with faucet designers, manufacturers, retailers and plumbers. Here's what we learned.

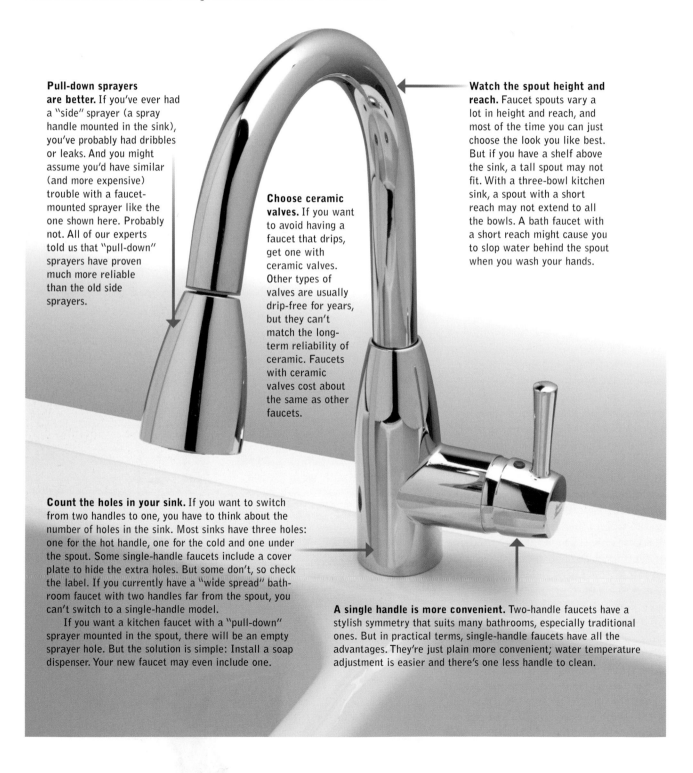

Pull-down sprayers are better. If you've ever had a "side" sprayer (a spray handle mounted in the sink), you've probably had dribbles or leaks. And you might assume you'd have similar (and more expensive) trouble with a faucet-mounted sprayer like the one shown here. Probably not. All of our experts told us that "pull-down" sprayers have proven much more reliable than the old side sprayers.

Choose ceramic valves. If you want to avoid having a faucet that drips, get one with ceramic valves. Other types of valves are usually drip-free for years, but they can't match the long-term reliability of ceramic. Faucets with ceramic valves cost about the same as other faucets.

Watch the spout height and reach. Faucet spouts vary a lot in height and reach, and most of the time you can just choose the look you like best. But if you have a shelf above the sink, a tall spout may not fit. With a three-bowl kitchen sink, a spout with a short reach may not extend to all the bowls. A bath faucet with a short reach might cause you to slop water behind the spout when you wash your hands.

Count the holes in your sink. If you want to switch from two handles to one, you have to think about the number of holes in the sink. Most sinks have three holes: one for the hot handle, one for the cold and one under the spout. Some single-handle faucets include a cover plate to hide the extra holes. But some don't, so check the label. If you currently have a "wide spread" bathroom faucet with two handles far from the spout, you can't switch to a single-handle model.

If you want a kitchen faucet with a "pull-down" sprayer mounted in the spout, there will be an empty sprayer hole. But the solution is simple: Install a soap dispenser. Your new faucet may even include one.

A single handle is more convenient. Two-handle faucets have a stylish symmetry that suits many bathrooms, especially traditional ones. But in practical terms, single-handle faucets have all the advantages. They're just plain more convenient; water temperature adjustment is easier and there's one less handle to clean.

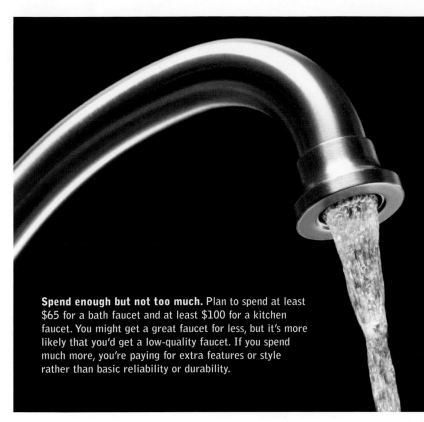

Spend enough but not too much. Plan to spend at least $65 for a bath faucet and at least $100 for a kitchen faucet. You might get a great faucet for less, but it's more likely that you'd get a low-quality faucet. If you spend much more, you're paying for extra features or style rather than basic reliability or durability.

Some finishes are tougher than others. Here's Rule No. 1 of faucet finishes: Choose a finish that matches nearby cabinet hardware, towel bars, etc. Mismatches look bad. If you plan to replace existing hardware, your choice of faucet finishes is wide open. The vast majority of faucets have polished chrome, satin nickel or bronze finishes. All of these finishes are durable and keep their good looks for years. But some are more durable than others.

Chrome is the most durable finish and the easiest to keep clean—that's why it's always been the favorite for commercial kitchens and public bathrooms. If your faucet gets heavy use, it's your best bet for long-term toughness.

Nickel finishes are usually labeled "brushed," "satin" or "stainless steel" and have a dull shine. They're durable but prone to fingerprints and water spots, so they're harder to keep clean. Some have a coating that reduces stains and smudges, but that coating isn't as durable as metal and may chip or wear.

Bronze faucets have a brownish tone and are often called "oiled" or "rubbed" bronze. But the surface is a coating (such as epoxy) rather than metal. This coating is tough stuff, but can be chipped or scratched more easily than metal.

Recessed lights upgrade

Dissatisfied with the look of the recessed lights in your kitchen or bathroom? You can change them in a few minutes just by changing the trim.

Remove the existing trim and bulb and look up inside the metal housing for a sticker with the brand name, the model number and compatible trim styles. If you can't find the information, or the brand isn't available, take the old trim to a lighting store and look for matches. Most manufacturers have several different types and sizes of housing that will accept a variety of trim styles.

Changing old, yellowed trim for new trim is simple—just pull out the old trim and attach the new trim in the same hooks. You can also replace standard trim with an eyeball-style trim that can be aimed in different directions, but it takes an extra step.

First, turn off the switch and circuit breaker and remove the bulb. Unscrew the wing nut that holds the base of the light in

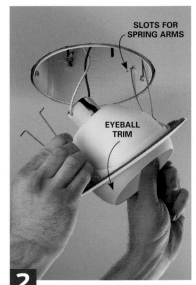

1 Remove the metal base from the housing, then pinch the spring clamps that hold the ceramic light socket in place.

SOCKET

2 Slide the spring-loaded metal arms up into the slots in the housing, then push the trim up against the ceiling and put the lightbulb in.

SLOTS FOR SPRING ARMS

EYEBALL TRIM

place and remove the socket (Photo 1). Then snap the socket into the top of the eyeball shroud and push the eyeball trim up into the can (Photo 2). Be sure to use the type of bulb recommended on the label in the housing.

WHAT IT TAKES

Time: 1 day
Skill level: Beginner

1 Swing-out shelf

Get everything within reach! This spacious, double-level shelving unit pivots in and out effortlessly.

2 Mini rollout

No more tipping! This rollout has taller sides for taller products as well as full-extension hardware.

3 Drawer top trays

Get organized! Make these nifty sliding trays for all your vanity drawers.

3 one-day vanity upgrades

Most vanities are poor storage spaces because they're designed for the convenience of plumbers, not for you. While that big, open box is nice for installing pipes, it leaves you with jumbled storage and wasted space.

But you can convert that box into useful space by installing any or all of these three upgrades. You'll expand the real estate under your sink and make it easy to find anything in seconds. Even a beginning DIYer can build all three projects in two or three days, for under $100.

① Swing-out shelf

Here's the answer to all that inaccessible clutter on the floor of your vanity. With one pull, you can bring stored items out of the dark recesses and into easy reach.

Chances are, the measurements shown in Figure A won't be best for your vanity. The surest way to determine the right size for your shelf is to cut a quarter circle from cardboard and test the fit. If your vanity has double doors, you can still build this shelf, but you may need to open both doors to swing it out. Here are some tips for building your swing-out shelf:

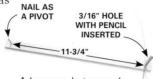

NAIL AS A PIVOT

3/16" HOLE WITH PENCIL INSERTED

11-3/4"

A homemade trammel is perfect for marking out the curved shelves.

■ To make the curved shelves, just mark a half circle and then cut it into two equal quarter circles.

■ A pneumatic brad nailer makes assembly a cinch. If you don't have a brad nailer, use trim screws. The awkward shape of the shelves makes hand-nailing difficult. Whether you use nails or screws, also use glue.

■ You can finish your shelf with a couple of coats of polyurethane. A can of spray lacquer is also a good option.

■ Piano hinges come in various lengths, but you probably won't find exactly what you need for your shelf. That's OK; You can cut it to length with a hacksaw.

Figure A

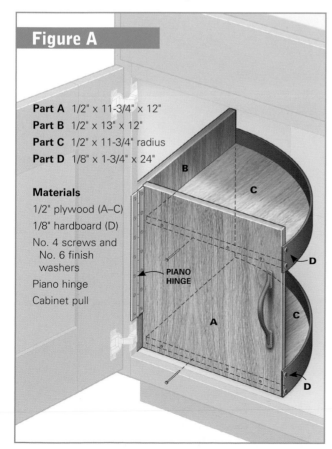

Part A 1/2" x 11-3/4" x 12"
Part B 1/2" x 13" x 12"
Part C 1/2" x 11-3/4" radius
Part D 1/8" x 1-3/4" x 24"

Materials

1/2" plywood (A–C)

1/8" hardboard (D)

No. 4 screws and No. 6 finish washers

Piano hinge

Cabinet pull

B

C

D

PIANO HINGE

A

C

D

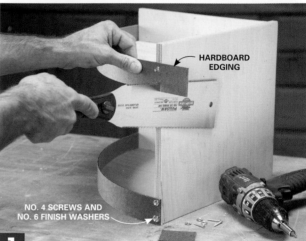

HARDBOARD EDGING

NO. 4 SCREWS AND NO. 6 FINISH WASHERS

1 Install the edging, then trim it. Cut the hardboard edging a few inches too long, fasten it with screws and slice off the excess with a fine-tooth saw. Finish washers give the screws a neater look.

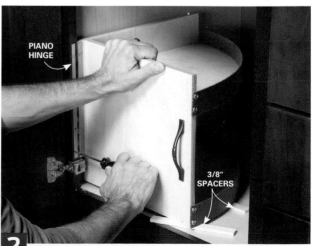

PIANO HINGE

3/8" SPACERS

2 Hang it on a hinge. Raise the shelf with spacers and align the shelf back with the inside edge of the face frame. Screw the piano hinge to the shelf back, then to the cabinet. You may have to notch the shelf back to clear the door hinge.

2 Mini rollout

This handy little rollout has tall sides, fronts and backs to keep bottles and cleaners in place as you open it. Alter the dimensions given in Figure B to suit your needs. Here are some building tips:

■ Assemble the drawer boxes with glue plus trim screws, finish nails or brad nails.

■ Shown is a 14-in. "full-extension" drawer slide. This type of slide is typically mounted on the side of a drawer, but it also works well as a light-duty undermount slide. If your home center doesn't carry full-extension slides in the length you need, go to any online cabinet hardware supplier. You can use a standard undermount slide, but your tray won't extend fully.

■ Finish the rollout with two coats of polyurethane or spray lacquer.

■ If you add a cabinet pull as shown here, be sure to set the base back a bit so the vanity door can close.

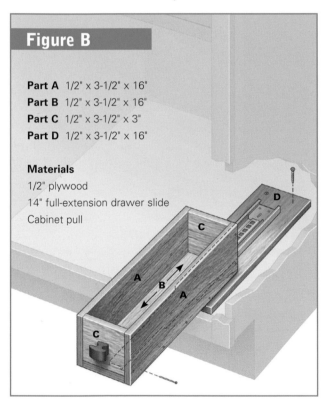

Figure B

Part A 1/2" x 3-1/2" x 16"
Part B 1/2" x 3-1/2" x 16"
Part C 1/2" x 3-1/2" x 3"
Part D 1/2" x 3-1/2" x 16"

Materials

1/2" plywood
14" full-extension drawer slide
Cabinet pull

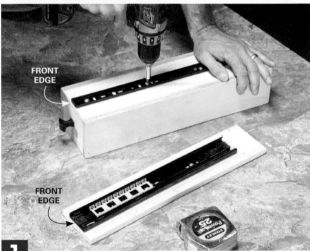

1 Mount the drawer slides. Separate the two parts of the drawer slide. Screw them to the tray and the base, aligned flush at the fronts.

FRONT EDGE

FRONT EDGE

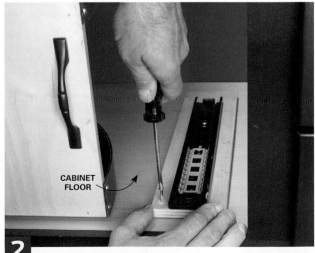

CABINET FLOOR

2 Elevate the drawer slide with a separate base. Fasten the tray base to the cabinet floor with No. 6 x 1-in. screws, then slide on the drawer.

familyhandyman.com

• Does your bathroom need an overhaul? Search for "bathroom remodel" to find complete step-by-step projects.

• Your feet will love a warm bathroom floor. Search for "in-floor heat" to see how to install an electric heat system.

• Drawer slides don't slide? Search for "drawer slide" to see how to replace them.

• Got bathroom clutter? We have tips and projects galore. Search for "bathroom storage."

• If this rollout is too small, search for "rollout" and get step-by-step instructions for a larger version.

• Old vanity top worn out? Glass tile makes an elegant, affordable replacement. And it's easier than you think. Search for "vanity top."

③ Drawer top tray

Drawers are often too deep for small bathroom stuff like razors, medicine and cosmetics. That means wasted space. These handy sliding trays reduce that waste and increase drawer real estate by 50 percent.

■ To size the tray, measure the drawer: Subtract 1/16 in. from the width of the drawer space and divide the length in half. Cut a piece of 1/8-in. hardboard this size.

■ You can make the tray any depth you like. If the opening in the vanity is taller than the height of the drawer, your tray can protrude above the drawer sides.

■ Finish the tray with a couple of coats of polyurethane or spray lacquer.

■ Stored items tend to slide around in the trays, so add shelf liner (available at home centers and discount stores).

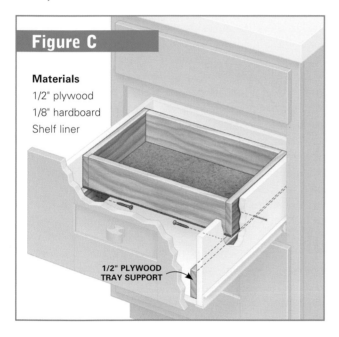

Figure C

Materials
1/2" plywood
1/8" hardboard
Shelf liner

1/2" PLYWOOD
TRAY SUPPORT

If you can get by without a vanity, a great way to make a small bathroom feel bigger is to replace the vanity with a stylish wall-hung sink. Visit familyhandyman.com and search "wall hung sink" for complete how-to instructions.

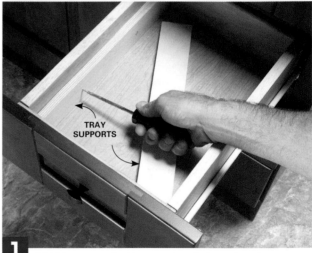

TRAY SUPPORTS

1 **Add tray supports.** Fasten strips of plywood to the drawer to support the tray. You only need two screws per support.

SHELF LINER

2 **Line the trays.** Cut shelf liner to fit the trays. Liner helps stored items stay put when you slide the tray.

Simple bathroom cabinet

In most bathrooms, a picture or small shelf hangs above the toilet. But you can make better use of that space with an attractive cabinet that offers about three times as much storage as a typical medicine cabinet.

The simple joinery and store-bought doors make this a great project for a woodworking novice. Assembling the crown and base can be a bit tricky, but the photos show that process, too.

The total materials bill for this cabinet was about $150. You'll need a miter saw to cut the trim. A table saw and a brad nailer save time, but you can make all the cuts with a circular saw and drive the nails by hand if you prefer.

The height and width of your cabinet may differ slightly from this one, depending on the bifold doors available at your home center. So choose your doors first and then alter the lengths of the sides, top, bottom and middle shelves if necessary. Bifold closet doors are sold as a pair, usually joined by hinges. Each of the doors shown here measured 11-15/16 in. wide, and were cut to length as shown in the photo in the sidebar on p. 46.

The easy-to-install hinges used here are available at home centers or online. All the other tools and materials, including the cabinet doors, are available at home centers. You may not find the exact same crown and base moldings used here, but most home centers carry a similar profile. Any 2-1/4-in. crown molding is appropriate for this project. For a more contemporary look, you can skip the crown and base altogether, since they're purely decorative.

Build a basic box

Cut the plywood parts to size. The dimensions used here are given in the Cutting List (p. 45). To make the short end cuts, use the homemade guide shown in Photo 3 and described below.

Assemble the cabinet box with glue and screws, followed by wood dowels for extra strength (Photo 1). You can buy long dowels and cut them into short pieces, but dowels precut and fluted for woodworking are easier to work with. This assembly method is quick, easy and strong. But because it requires lots of wood filler to hide the fasteners, it's for painted work only. If you want to use stain and a clear finish, biscuits or pocket screws are a better choice.

Drill 1/8-in. pilot and countersink holes for the screws using a drill bit that does both at once. Attach the top, bottom and cleats to one side, then add the other side. Mark the middle shelf position on the sides, slip it into place and fasten it (there's no need for glue).

Before you drill the dowel holes, make sure the box is square by taking diagonal measurements; equal measurements mean the box is square. If necessary, screw a strip of plywood diagonally across the back of the box to hold it square. For clean, splinter-free holes, drill the dowel holes with a 3/8-in. brad-point bit, making the holes 1/8 in. deeper than the length of the dowels. That way, you can sink the dowels below the surface of the plywood and fill the holes with wood filler. With the box completed, drill holes for the adjustable shelf supports (Photo 2) using a brad-point drill bit. Most shelf supports require a 1/4-in. hole.

Cut and hang the doors

Cut the doors using a saw guide (Photo 3). To make a guide, screw a straight 1x3 to a 14 x 18-in. scrap of 3/4-in. plywood. Then run your saw along the 1x3 to cut off the excess plywood and create a guide that steers your saw perfectly straight and indicates the exact path of the cut. Simply mark the doors, align the guide with the marks, clamp it in place and cut.

Screw the hinges to the doors 3 in. from the ends (Photo 4). The fronts and backs of louvered doors look similar, so check twice before you drill. Stand the doors against the cabinet, setting them on spacers to create a 1/8-in. gap at the bottom. The gap between the doors should also be about 1/8 in. Clamp each door in position and screw the hinges in place (Photo 5). If the doors don't align perfectly because the box is slightly out-of-square, don't worry. You can square the box when you hang it. The hinges also adjust up or down 1/16 in.

Figure A
Bathroom cabinet

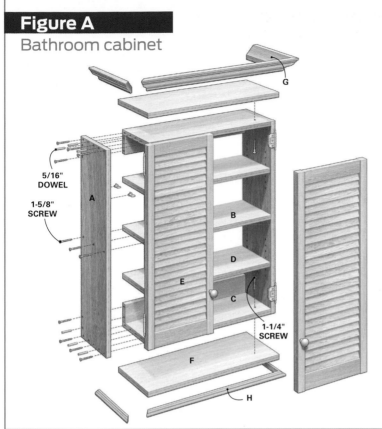

5/16" DOWEL

1-5/8" SCREW

A

B

C

D

E

F

G

H

1-1/4" SCREW

Materials List

ITEM	QTY.
4' x 8' x 3/4" birch plywood	1
2-1/4"-wide crown molding	5'
3/4"-tall base cap molding	5'
1-1/4" screws	1 box
1-5/8" screws	1 box
5/16" or 3/8" dowels	16
1-1/2" finish nails	1 box
Hinges	4
Shelf supports	8
Spray primer	1 can
Spray paint	2 cans
Wood glue	
Wood filler	

Cutting List

KEY	QTY.	SIZE & DESCRIPTION
A	2	8" x 32-5/8" sides
B	3	8" x 22-1/2" top, bottom and middle shelf
C	2	3" x 22-1/2" top and bottom cleats
D	2	8" x 22-1/4" adjustable shelves
E	2	11-15/16" x 32-3/8" doors
F	2	9" x 24" crown and base frames
G	3	2-1/4"-wide crown molding (cut to fit)
H	3	3/4"-tall base molding (cut to fit)

Except for moldings, all parts are 3/4-in. plywood.

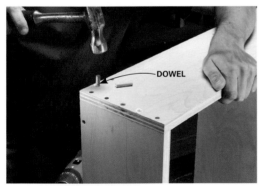

DOWEL

1 Assemble the cabinet box quickly with glue and wood screws. Then add glued dowels for rock-solid joints. Drill splinter-free dowel holes with a brad-point bit.

WHAT IT TAKES

Time: 1 day
Skill level: Intermediate

BRAD-POINT BIT

DEPTH MARKER

2 Drill shelf support holes using a scrap of pegboard to position the holes. Wrap masking tape around the drill bit so you don't drill all the way through.

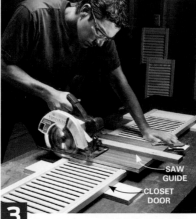

SAW GUIDE

CLOSET DOOR

3 Cut the doors using a homemade saw guide to ensure a straight cut. Lay the door face down so any splintering takes place on the back of the door.

SELF-CENTERING BIT

4 Mount the hinges on the doors. A self-centering drill bit positions the screw holes for perfectly placed hinges.

5 Position the doors carefully and clamp them to the cabinet. Then screw the hinges to the cabinet from inside for a foolproof, exact fit.

HOLD-DOWN BLOCK

6 Cut the crown molding upside down and leaning against the fence. Clamp a block to the saw's fence so you can hold the molding firmly against the fence.

7 Nail the crown to the frame. Nail the mitered corners only if necessary. If they fit tight and are perfectly aligned, let the glue alone hold them together.

CROWN

BASE

8 Center the crown on the cabinet and fasten it with screws driven from inside. Then center the cabinet on the base and attach it the same way.

Add the crown and base

Measure the top of the cabinet (including the doors) and cut the plywood crown and base frames to that size. Set your miter saw to 45 degrees and cut the crown molding upside down, leaning against the fence (Photo 6). Also miter a "tester" section of molding to help you position the sidepieces when you nail them in place. To avoid splitting, be sure to predrill nail holes.

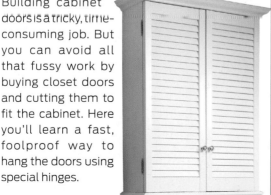

Store-bought closet doors keep it fast and simple

Building cabinet doors is a tricky, time-consuming job. But you can avoid all that fussy work by buying closet doors and cutting them to fit the cabinet. Here you'll learn a fast, foolproof way to hang the doors using special hinges.

With the sides in place, add the front piece of crown molding. Cut it slightly long and then "shave" one end with your miter saw until it fits perfectly. Add the molding to the base frame the same way. Screw both the crown and base to the cabinet (Photo 8).

A quick finish

Brushing paint onto louvered doors is slow, fussy work, but you can avoid that hassle by using aerosol-can primer and paint. First, remove the doors and hinges. Cover the dowels, nails and screw heads with wood filler and sand the filler smooth. Also fill any voids in the plywood's edges. Sand the cabinet box, crown, base and doors with 120-grit paper. Spray all the parts with a white stain-blocking primer (such as BIN, Cover Stain or KILZ). When the primer dries, sand it lightly with a fine sanding sponge. Finally, spray on at least two coats of spray paint. High-gloss paint will accentuate every tiny surface flaw, so consider using satin or matte.

To hang the cabinet, locate studs and drive two 3-in. screws through the top cleat. Then rehang the doors. Close the doors to check their fit. Nudge the bottom of the cabinet left or right to square it and align the doors. Then drive screws through the bottom cleat.

Upcycled router table

An old chunk of countertop and 40 bucks' worth of hardware

WHAT IT TAKES

Time: 1 day
Skill level: Intermediate

This homemade router table is tough, easy to take to job sites and easy to store. The best feature is the screw-on fence face. In two minutes, you can switch to a face with a larger hole for larger bits or a super-tall face for vertical routing. And since it's replaceable, you can drive screws into it to secure featherboards or guides.

The only tricky part is cutting the hole for the router plate, so this article will focus on a goof-proof method for that. For the rest of the project, cut and assemble the parts as shown in Figure A.

The table

The first step is to cut up the section of countertop. Some countertops have a hump just above the rounded front edge. If yours does, you'll have to cut off a couple of inches and lose the finished front edge. Next, cut off the backsplash. Lay the countertop upside down and clamp on a straight board to guide your circular saw. You can make the other cuts with a circular saw or table saw. Keep in mind that saw teeth leave chips as they exit plastic laminate. To avoid chipping, cut with the laminate

Figure A
Router table fence

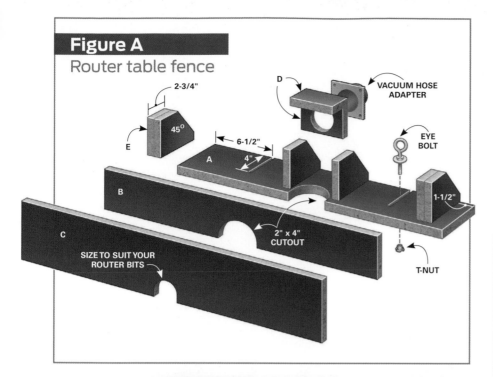

- 2-3/4"
- 45°
- E
- D
- VACUUM HOSE ADAPTER
- 6-1/2"
- 4"
- A
- B
- EYE BOLT
- 2" x 4" CUTOUT
- 1-1/2"
- C
- SIZE TO SUIT YOUR ROUTER BITS
- T-NUT

Materials List

KEY	QTY.	SIZE & DESCRIPTION
A	1	6" x 28" base
B	1	3-1/2" x 28" face backer
C	1	5" x 30" face
D	2	2-3/4" x 4-1/2" dust pen
E	6	3-1/2" x 5-3/16" brackets

All parts are cut from 3/4-in. particleboard covered with plastic laminate. The table (not shown) is 20-1/2 x 36 in. The steel rails that support the table are 34 in. long.

Stuff you'll need

Countertop: At least 6 linear feet to build a 3-ft.-long table. Go Dumpster-diving or check the bargain bin at a home center ($0 to $40).

Metal rails: If you can't find a bed frame to cut up, buy 6 ft. of 1-in. angle.

FENDER WASHER

NUT

T-nuts, washers and eye bolts: We used 3/8-in. hardware, but anything over 1/4 in. will do.

EYE BOLT

T-NUTS

Vacuum port: Use a rubber vacuum hose adapter.

VACUUM HOSE ADAPTER

Miscellaneous: A 1/2-in. pattern router bit with bearing at the top, router table insert plate, wood glue, coarse-thread screws (1/2, 1-1/4, 2 in.).

PATTERN BIT

1 **Build a guide for routing the plate opening.** Screw the plate to the table and assemble a two-layer guide around the plate. Place washers along two sides of the plate so the guide opening is slightly larger than the plate.

WASHER

ROUTER PLATE

2 **Rout a groove first.** Clamp down the long ends of the frame, remove the plate and cut a groove with a pattern bit. The bearing guides the bit perfectly along the inside of the guide.

3 **Cut out the plate opening, leaving a lip.** Drill a starter hole for the blade and cut along the inside of the groove with a jigsaw. That will leave a perfect lip to support the plate.

4 **Add the rails and T-nuts.** Stiffen the table with metal rails and hammer in the T-nuts that will lock down the fence.

face up on a table saw or face down with a circular saw. A cut laminate edge is sharp enough to slice skin. To dull those sharp edges, make a few quick passes with sandpaper.

After the table's cut to size, create a hole for the router insert plate. Place the insert plate 3-1/2 in. from the back edge of the table and build a guide around it (Photo 1). This guide is 1/2 in. thick, perfect for a 1-in.-long pattern bit. For a shorter or longer bit, use thicker or thinner material. Before cutting the groove (Photo 2), set the router bit depth. Stack two scraps of the guide material and the plate. Set your router on the plate and adjust the depth. To finish the hole, cut along the inner edge of the groove (Photo 3).

The fence

Build the fence as shown in Figure A. Assemble the fence with screws and glue where particleboard meets particleboard; screws alone where plastic laminate meets particleboard. Drill pilot holes and use coarse-thread screws; fine-thread screws won't hold. To cut the slots in the fence base (A), drill 1/2-in. holes and then cut with a jigsaw. Two of the fence brackets (E) are double thick. To make them, glue scraps together back to back and then cut them to size. The size of the dust pen hole depends on the size of your vacuum hose. You can buy a rubber vacuum hose adapter and cut off the stepped end. To fasten the fence face, drive 1-1/2-in. screws through the backer (B) into the face. Before you drill the T-nut holes and install the T-nuts (Photo 4), mark their locations using the fence base as a guide.

Perfect for a crowded shop

This router table is bigger than most but takes up less storage space because it isn't mounted on legs or a cabinet. To use the table, lay it across sawhorses. To store it, hang it on a wall or slip it into any narrow space.

Choosing a plate

Insert plates made for router tables start at about $30 for a basic model like the one shown here. Search online to browse a huge selection. For about half the price, you can also make your own plate from an acrylic sheet (at least 1/4 in. thick; sold at home centers)—but the manufactured version may give better results with less fuss. If it isn't perfectly flat, give it a couple of days of corrective clamping and it flattens nicely.

familyhandyman.com
- Search for "router" and get expert tips for using routers and tables.
- Workshop crowded and crammed? Search for "shop storage" to maximize your space.
- Turn your table saw into a precision crosscutting machine. Search for "table saw sled" to find three great sled designs—or check out the one on the next page.

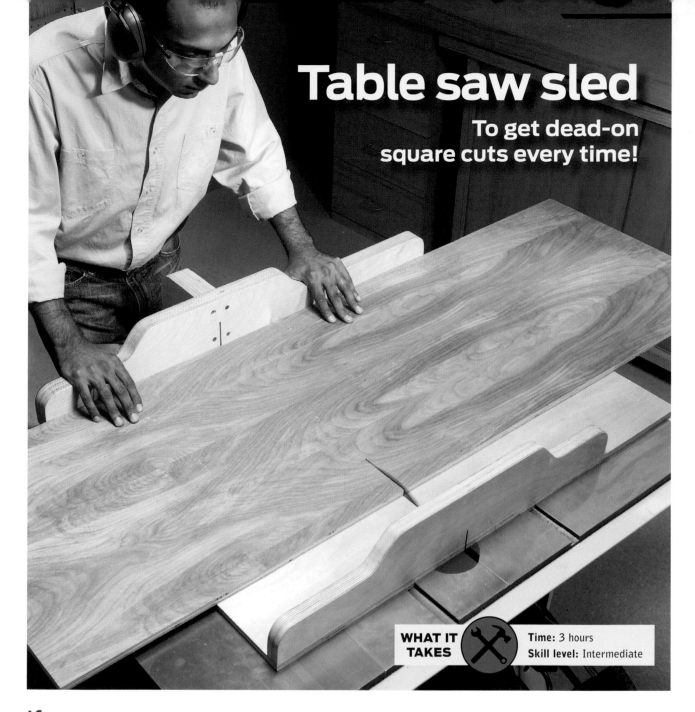

Table saw sled
To get dead-on square cuts every time!

WHAT IT TAKES — **Time:** 3 hours · **Skill level:** Intermediate

If you own a table saw, you know it works great for ripping long pieces. But did you know that you can crosscut wide pieces with the same ease and accuracy? All it takes is a table saw sled. A table saw sled rides in the miter gauge slots and has a fence that's mounted exactly 90 degrees to the blade, enabling accurate square cuts. We'll show you how to build a sled using a 42-in. square sheet of 1/2-in. plywood.

We used top-quality nine-ply birch, but any flat plywood with smooth faces will work. The tricky parts of the construction are cutting runners that slide smoothly in the tracks, and getting the fence perfectly square to the blade. We'll show you how to accomplish both as you construct the sled.

Start by cutting strips of plywood for the stiffener, front fence and blade cover (Figure A). Cut them 1/4 in.

wider and 1/2 in. longer than the finished size to allow for trimming. Then spread wood glue on the mating faces and clamp them together. Clamp them onto a perfectly flat surface like the top of your table saw. Try to keep the layers lined up as you clamp them. After about 20 minutes, scrape off the partially hardened glue. Then run the pieces through the table saw, removing about 1/4 in. Using Figure A as a guide, mark the shapes onto the pieces and saw them out with a jigsaw. Smooth the curves with a belt sander.

The next step is to cut the runners from strips of hardwood. If you have standard 3/4-in.-wide miter gauge slots, sand or plane a 1x3 hardwood board until it slides easily in the slots (Photo 1). (For narrower slots, you'll have to plane or cut the 1x3 to reduce its thickness.) Then rip strips from the 1x3 that are about 1/16 in.

thinner than the depth of the slot. Photos 2 and 3 show how to attach the strips to the sled base. Let the glue set for about 20 minutes. Then remove the assembly from the table saw and scrape off excess glue from the edges of the runners and bottom of the base. You'll also have to clean out any glue that has gotten into the slots on the table saw. Slide the sled back and forth in the slots. If the sled doesn't slide easily, inspect the runners for darkened areas where the metal has rubbed on the wood. Use spray adhesive to attach a piece of 80-grit sandpaper to a square-edged block of wood and sand the darkened areas to remove a little wood (Photo 4). Repeat this process until the sled slides freely.

Glue and screw the stiffener to the front edge of the base, being careful to keep screws away from the path of the table saw blade. Then set the table saw blade to about 3/4 in. high and slide the base into the blade. Stop cutting when you get within 3 in. of the back of the base. Turn off the saw and let it come to a stop before removing the sled. Align the fence with the back edge of the base and drive a screw into the right end. Photo 5 shows how to square the fence to the saw blade and clamp it in place. Screw the blade cover to the back of the fence, being careful to keep the screws well away from the path of the blade.

Test the cut

With the clamp firmly in place, set a 12-in. or wider scrap of plywood on the sled and cut it in two. Test the accuracy of the sled by flipping one side of the cut scrap over and pushing the freshly cut edge against the other half (Photo 6). If the two pieces fit perfectly with no gap, the sled is cutting squarely and you can drive three additional screws into the fence to hold it in place. Otherwise, tap the clamped end of the fence with a hammer to nudge the fence a bit. Then make another test cut. Repeat this process until the cut is perfect. Then add the screws.

Complete the sled by adding the stop blocks. With the blade half covered by the fence and blade cover, screw a block to the bottom of the sled. Use carriage bolts to attach another stop block to the table saw bed (Photo 7).

CAUTION

You must remove the blade guard on your table saw to use the sled. To prevent accidents:

- Adjust the blade so that no more than 1/4 in. is exposed above the board you're sawing.
- Keep your hands well away from the path of the blade.
- After completing a cut, turn off the saw and let the blade come to a complete stop before moving the sled.

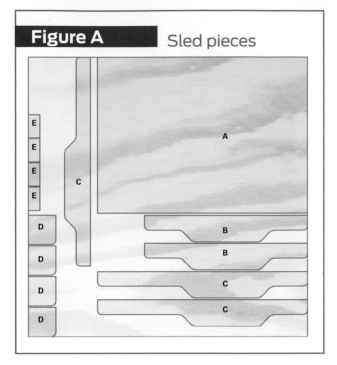

Figure A Sled pieces

Materials List

ITEM

42" x 42" x 1/2" plywood

3/4" x 2-1/2" x 3' hardwood board

Eleven 1-1/2" screws

Four 3" screws

Two 2" carriage bolts and nuts (for stop block)

Wood glue

Cutting List

KEY	QTY.	SIZE & DESCRIPTION
A	1	32" x 24" x 1/2" base
B	2	24" x 4" x 1/2" stiffener
C	3	32" x 4" x 1/2" fence
D	4	4" x 4" x 1/2" blade guard
E	4	1-1/2" x 3-1/2" stop block

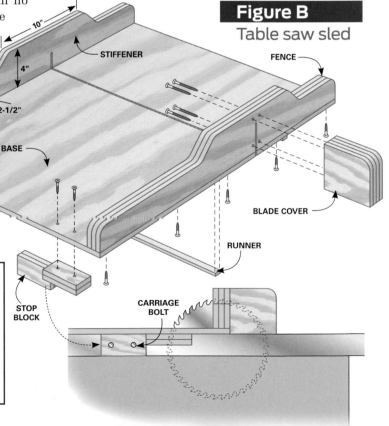

Figure B Table saw sled

1 Slide a hardwood board in the miter gauge slot on your table saw to check the fit. If it's too tight, sand and plane it until it slides easily with no slop. Work on this while you're waiting for the glue to set up on the fence blank (about a half hour).

FENCE BLANK

MITER GAUGE SLOT

2 Rest the runners on pennies to elevate the top edge above the surface of the saw. Apply a thin bead of wood glue down the center of the top of the runners.

RUNNER

3 Glue the base to the runner, using the table saw fence to position it. Make sure the edge farthest from the fence overhangs the table saw at least 2 in. Set weights on the base until the glue dries.

BUTT AGAINST FENCE

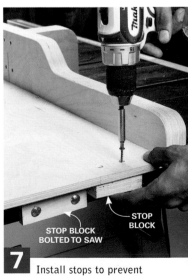

4 Sand the edges of the runners where they rub on the sides of the miter gauge slots. Dark spots indicate areas that need sanding.

80-GRIT SANDPAPER

OAK RUNNER

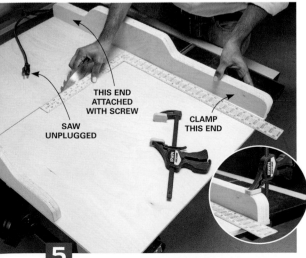

5 Square the fence with the blade. Raise the blade and press a framing square against it. Swivel the fence on a single screw in one end, and clamp the opposite end when the fence is square to the blade.

THIS END ATTACHED WITH SCREW

SAW UNPLUGGED

CLAMP THIS END

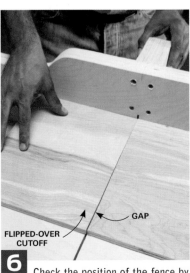

6 Check the position of the fence by cutting a scrap of plywood. Flip one side over and butt the two pieces together. A gap means the fence isn't square.

FLIPPED-OVER CUTOFF

GAP

7 Install stops to prevent the blade from cutting through the blade cover.

STOP BLOCK BOLTED TO SAW

STOP BLOCK

Drum sander table

If you don't want to pop for a dedicated oscillating drum sander, a sanding drum chucked into a drill press is a quick way to sand contours. But unlike the real deal, there's no dust collection, and since the drum doesn't oscillate up and down, only the lower edge of the sanding surface gets used. It also means there's always a little gap where the drum is slightly above the drill press table. This simple sander table solves all these problems automatically.

Use 1/4-in. or any other thickness plywood for the base, and size it slightly smaller than the drill press table so you can clamp it down. Build a 1x4 frame, a few inches smaller than the base, so there's room for the clamps, and glue and pin it to the frame. Then glue and nail 3/4-in. material to the frame for the top. This one is 16 in. square. Build it longer or deeper if you want to sand wider or longer stuff. Cover the top with plastic laminate if you wish. It's worth the trouble because using a drum sander is tricky, and the slippery surface makes it much easier to control sanding.

Finally, drill a hole slightly larger than the drum in the center of the top and a dust-port hole in the frame sized to fit your shop vacuum hose. Move the drill press table up and down to use the entire sanding surface as it wears.

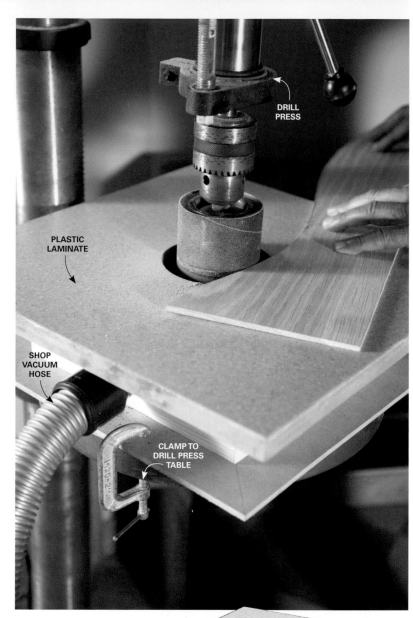

DRILL PRESS

PLASTIC LAMINATE

SHOP VACUUM HOSE

CLAMP TO DRILL PRESS TABLE

Drum-sanding ABCs

The biggest mistake drum-sander neophytes make is to remove too much material on each pass. Don't be overly aggressive: Use coarse grits only when necessary, and use very light pressure on each pass. Feel for imperfections with your fingertips, and mark the high spots with a pencil.

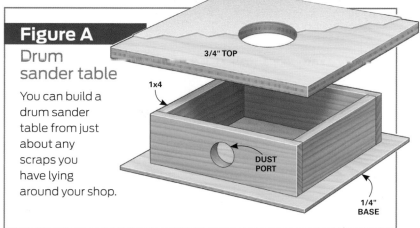

Figure A
Drum sander table

You can build a drum sander table from just about any scraps you have lying around your shop.

3/4" TOP

1x4

DUST PORT

1/4" BASE

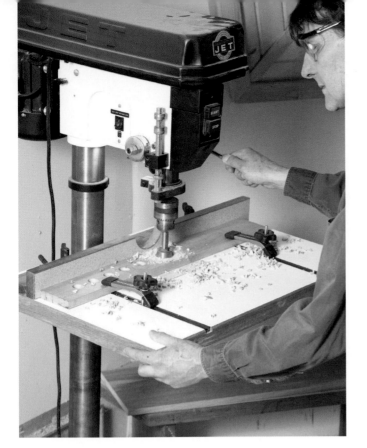

Drill press table

Drill presses are designed for working with metal, not wood, but you can adapt them with this dedicated woodworking drill press table, complete with dadoes, plastic laminate and T-tracks.

Here's an overview of the construction process. Glue 1-in. oversized particleboard panels together, then cut them to size on the table saw. Edge-band both sides of the table, then belt-sand the top so the hardwood is flush with the surfaces. Cut the laminate squares 1 in. oversize and apply them with contact cement. Then rout the laminate squares flush with a flush-trim bit and chamfer them with a 45-degree bit. Rout out the 1/2-in.-deep recess for the throat plate.

Cut the 3/4-in.-wide dadoes on the table saw. Cut the clearance hole on the fence with a 2-1/2-in. hole saw on the drill press. Screw the fence together before applying the laminate, then rout that as you did with the tabletop.

Lag screws (1-1/2 x 5/16 in.) and washers work great for securing your new top to the existing drill press table. The instructions with the T-track will tell you the rest.

Bells and whistles

A Fence: A semicircular clearance hole for the chuck allows for drilling holes that are close to the fence.

B Throat plate: An inset 1/2-in. replaceable throat plate takes the abuse so the top won't have to.

C T-tracks: T-tracks are universally useful gizmos that allow you to endlessly adjust jigs, fences and hold-downs. On this table, they're used for a sliding fence and hold-downs.

D Laminate: Plastic laminate on both the top and bottom will keep the top from warping with humidity changes.

E Edging: A hardwood edge protects the rather delicate core from getting dinged up—plus, it's pretty.

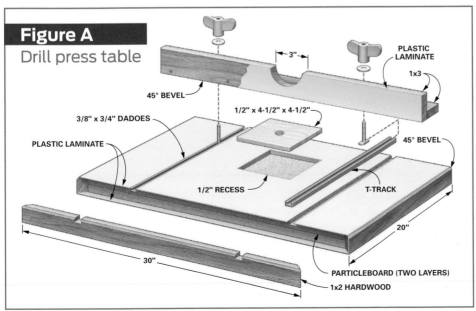

Figure A
Drill press table

- 45° BEVEL
- 3/8" x 3/4" DADOES
- PLASTIC LAMINATE
- 1/2" x 4-1/2" x 4-1/2"
- 3"
- PLASTIC LAMINATE
- 1x3
- 45° BEVEL
- 1/2" RECESS
- T-TRACK
- 20"
- 30"
- PARTICLEBOARD (TWO LAYERS)
- 1x2 HARDWOOD

Materials List

Table: Two 2-ft. squares of particleboard. (You can get 2x2s at most home centers or have them cut from full sheets.)

Edge band: 8 lin. ft. of 1x2 hardwood.

Fence: 6 lin. ft. of 1x3 hardwood.

Laminate: Buy the smallest size sheet that'll give you two 20 x 30-in. pieces at the home center for anywhere between $20 and $50.

T-Track parts: You'll need two each of these: 24-in. tracks, hold-down clamps, knobs and 2-1/2-in. T-Slot bolts. (These parts cost a total of about $50 and are available at woodworking stores or online.)

Garage storage wall

Plastic storage bins
and simple shelves turn
chaos into order

WHAT IT TAKES

Time: 1 day
Skill level: Beginner

BEFORE

Here's a quick, easy-on-the-wallet solution: simple shelves that can hold plastic storage bins. You can build the whole project in less than a day, for about $300 for 26 ft. of shelving (the bins were extra).

This is what the garage looked like before the storage system—look familiar?

SATURDAY, 10 A.M.

1 **Mark the frame parts for quick assembly.** Cut all your frame parts to length. Then mark where the rails are going to be screwed to each leg. Do the same thing to the 2x2s. This makes the whole thing go together in a snap.

RAIL LOCATION

10:45 A.M.

2 **Assemble the frames.** Working on top of a sheet of plywood helps keep each frame squared up. Use the edges of the plywood to line up and adjust things as you screw the frame together. It also really helps to pick the straightest lumber possible when you're shopping.

2:30 P.M.

3 **Screw on the shelves.** Installing the shelves in each frame is a lot easier if you have a helper to hold the frames. If you're working alone, lean one of the frames against the wall and hold up the other frame while you screw the first shelf into place.

Materials List

(To build one shelf unit 95-1/4 in. long x 80 in. high)

- Two 8' 1x2s
- Eight 8' 2x2s
- Eight 7' 2x4s
- Two 4' x 8' x 3/4" BC plywood sheets
- Masking tape and construction screws (1-1/2", 2-1/2" and 5")

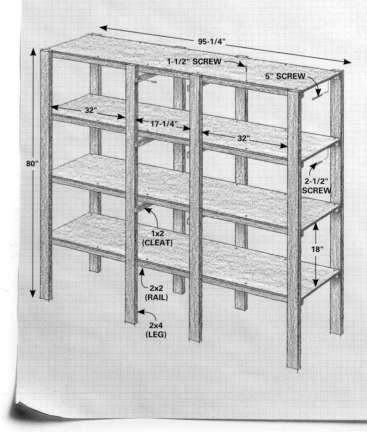

95-1/4"

1-1/2" SCREW

5" SCREW

32"

17-1/4"

32"

80"

2-1/2" SCREW

1x2 (CLEAT)

18"

2x2 (RAIL)

2x4 (LEG)

Tips

■ Each storage unit is basically two frames tied together with plywood shelves. Buy your bins first so you can customize the height and depth of each shelf space. Remember to leave enough clearance space in front of your shelving units to open your car doors.

■ Small bins are great for storing screws, glue and painting supplies in the middle bays of each unit. The best bins for hanging are those with snap-lock lids. They allow you to hang heavier loads without worrying that the lid will come off.

■ The fussiest measurements are those for the center bay of smaller bins. If your width measurements are off by a quarter-inch, the bins won't sit squarely between the cleats or will be too tight to slide easily.

■ If your garage floor sometimes gets wet, nail plastic feet to the bottom of the legs. (A set of four nail-on plastic feet costs about $3 at home centers.)

■ You can paint the wood to give it a classy look or leave it bare. Painting it before you put it together is a lot easier than painting it once it's assembled.

1:30 P.M.

TAPE MARKS STUDS

5" CONSTRUCTION SCREW

4 **Fasten the shelves to the wall.** Screw each unit to the wall through the top rail using self-tapping lag screws (GRK is one brand) spaced every second or third stud. This shelf unit is really sturdy. But make it ultra-secure by screwing the units together through the front legs. Shim the legs if your floor is sloped or uneven.

3 P.M.

SPACER

CLEAT

5 **Install cleats for slide-out bins.** To avoid stacking the small bins on top of one another, hang the top bins from cleats. Installing the cleats goes really fast if you start your screws in each cleat first and then use a spacer to mark the cleat's location as you screw it on.

I.D. bins the smart way

Think about how you'd like to identify the contents of each storage bin. Some people use adhesive labels or write with markers directly on the bins. The best system lets you make changes easily. We like the adhesive storage pouches that come with cardboard inserts (or you can just use index cards). Changing the label is as easy as slipping a new card into the pouch. Check office supply stores or search online.

CHAPTER

4 Outdoor projects

Mix-and-match planters

Build planters in a variety of styles— from one simple design

Building an attractive planter is easy with the method shown here. Each starts with a simple plywood box. Then you add a beveled cap, legs and siding to match your house, deck or patio. For extra durability and longevity, these planters are designed to accept standard size plastic liners to contain the moist soil.

The cost of the materials for the planters ranges from $50 to $80, depending on what you choose for siding. You can complete each one in a day. Two power tools—a table saw and a power miter box—make this project much easier. Use the table saw to cut the bevel on the top cap and to rip the leg pieces to

width. A power miter box simplifies the task of getting tight-fitting miters on the top cap. You can also use it to make all the square cuts on the ends of legs and trim. Shop for the plastic liners first; if you can't find the exact size shown here, simply modify the planter dimensions to fit the ones you find. You'll find a wide variety at any home or garden center.

The core of each planter is a box of 3/4-in. CDX or BC plywood. Most home centers and lumberyards will sell you a partial sheet of plywood and cut it into easily manageable sizes for you to haul home. Cut plywood pieces to final

Lap siding planter (see p. 63)

Cedar shingle planter (see p. 64)

size with a table saw, or clamp a straightedge to the plywood and cut it with your circular saw. Assemble the box with water-resistant wood glue and 6d galvanized nails (Photo 1). Add plywood braces inside the long planter to square the box and hold the long sides straight. The braces shown here are centered, but you can shift them down if they obstruct the liner (Photo 2). The other two planters don't need braces if you make sure they're square after you assemble them. Check with a framing square and add braces if they're needed.

Shown here is 5/4x6 (1 in. x 5-1/2 in. actual dimensions) cedar decking for the legs, but you can substitute other 5/4 decking if cedar isn't available.

First rip the deck boards to 5-1/4 in. to remove the rounded corners on one edge. Then run the squared edge against the table saw fence when you rip the 3-in.- and 2-in.-wide leg pieces. Cut the pieces to length and glue and nail them together with 8d galvanized casing nails (Photo 3). Sand the saw marks from the board edges before you screw the assembled legs to the box.

Ripping the bevel on the 2x4 top cap may require you to remove the blade guard. If so, use extreme caution to keep your fingers well away from the blade. Make sure the blade is tilted away from the fence as shown in the photo. Mount a featherboard and use push sticks to complete the cut (Photo 5). Start the cut by pushing with your back hand while holding the board down with a push stick in your front hand. Keep a second push stick within easy reach. When your back hand gets to the rear edge of the table saw, pick up the second push stick and use it along with the front push stick to push the board clear past the saw blade. Keep your attention focused on the saw blade at all times. Shut off the saw and wait for the blade to stop before retrieving the beveled board.

Photo 6 shows how to assemble the top cap pieces into a frame that's easy to attach to the box. Start by

Buy your liners first and adjust the planter dimensions if necessary.

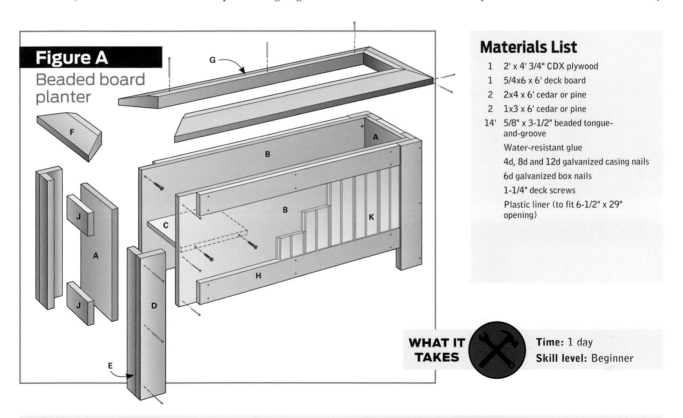

Figure A
Beaded board planter

Materials List

1	2' x 4' 3/4" CDX plywood
1	5/4x6 x 6' deck board
2	2x4 x 6' cedar or pine
2	1x3 x 6' cedar or pine
14'	5/8" x 3-1/2" beaded tongue-and-groove
	Water-resistant glue
	4d, 8d and 12d galvanized casing nails
	6d galvanized box nails
	1-1/4" deck screws
	Plastic liner (to fit 6-1/2" x 29" opening)

WHAT IT TAKES

Time: 1 day
Skill level: Beginner

Cutting List

KEY	QTY.	SIZE & DESCRIPTION
A	2	3/4" x 8" x 11-7/8" plywood ends
B	2	3/4" x 32" x 11-7/8" plywood sides
C	2	3/4" x 8" x 7-3/4" plywood braces
D	4	1" x 3" x 15" legs
E	4	1" x 2" x 15" legs

KEY	QTY.	SIZE & DESCRIPTION
F	2	1-1/2" x 3-1/2" x 13-1/2" beveled cap
G	2	1-1/2" x 3-1/2" x 36" beveled cap
H	4	3/4" x 2-1/2" x 28-1/2" trim (cut to fit)
J	4	3/4" x 2-1/2" x 6" trim (cut to fit)
K	22	5/8" x 3-1/4" x 6-7/8" beaded boards

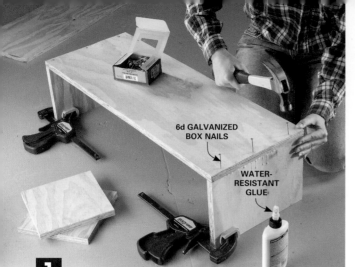

1 Cut the plywood sides to size and glue and nail the sides together. Use clamps to hold the sides upright.

6d GALVANIZED BOX NAILS

WATER-RESISTANT GLUE

2 Predrill screw clearance holes through the planter sides and screw in a plywood brace at each end. Center the brace.

1-1/4" DECK SCREWS

PLYWOOD BRACE

6"

3 Rip 5/4 decking material and cut it to length for the legs. Glue and nail a 3-in. piece to a 2-in. piece.

8d GALVANIZED CASING NAILS

D

E

PLANTER LEG

4 Set the plywood box on a flat surface and screw the leg assemblies to it. Make sure the legs are flush with the top of the planter box.

1-1/4" DECK SCREWS

TOP OF PLANTER

BOTTOM OF PLANTER

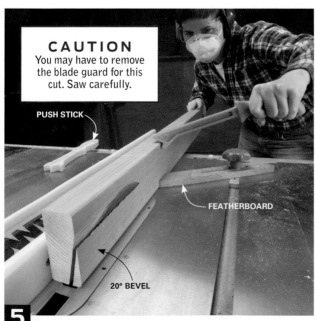

CAUTION
You may have to remove the blade guard for this cut. Saw carefully.

PUSH STICK

FEATHERBOARD

20° BEVEL

5 Rip a 20-degree bevel on the 2x4 tops with a table saw. Use a featherboard and push stick for extra safety.

gluing the miters and clamping one long side as shown. Then drill 1/8-in. pilot holes for the nails. Drive a pair of 8d galvanized casing nails from opposite sides at each corner to pin the miters together. Offset the nails slightly so they don't hit each other.

Mount the frame to the box by centering it with an even overhang all around and nailing it down with 12d galvanized casing nails (Photo 7). Measure and drill 5/32-in. pilot holes for the nails, making sure they're centered on the top edges of the plywood.

Add siding to complete the planter

Beaded board is great for a traditional-looking painted planter. For the best-looking planter, plan ahead and cut an equal amount from the first and last boards. Start by nailing the top trim (H) to the plywood box with 4d galvanized casing nails. Use a precut beaded board as a spacer to position the bottom board precisely. When you glue in the beaded boards, make sure to leave a 1/8-in. space at each end to allow room for expansion (Photo 8). Fill the space with caulk before painting.

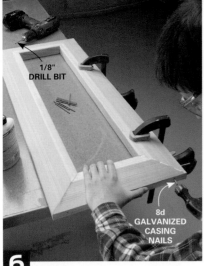

1/8" DRILL BIT

8d GALVANIZED CASING NAILS

6 Cut the cap pieces to length with 45-degree miters on the ends. Drill pilot holes for the nails. Then glue and nail the miters together.

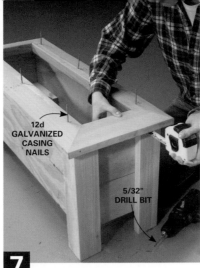

12d GALVANIZED CASING NAILS

5/32" DRILL BIT

7 Drill pilot holes and glue and nail the cap to the planter box. Measure to make sure the overhang is even on all sides.

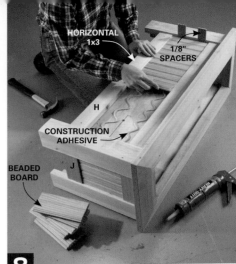

HORIZONTAL 1x3

1/8" SPACERS

H

CONSTRUCTION ADHESIVE

BEADED BOARD

J

8 Cut the trim pieces H and J to length and nail them to the top and bottom edges of the box. Cut beaded board to fit and glue the pieces onto the plywood with construction adhesive.

Lap siding planter

The tall box shown in the lower left corner on p. 60 is sided with 1/2-in. x 3-1/2-in. cedar lap siding. Simply cut the siding to fit between the legs. Rip a 1-in. strip off the thin edge of a siding piece for a starter. (Rip the leftover to fit at the top later.) Then nail the starter strips along the bottom of the plywood (under the first row of siding) to hold the first piece of siding at the correct angle. Predrill 1/16-in. holes 3/4 in. from the end and 5/8 in. from the bottom of each piece to prevent splitting. Then nail on the siding with 4d galvanized box nails. The top cap on this planter fits flush to the inside edge of the plywood box, which may cause the nails protruding through the inside to interfere with the plastic liner. If so, bend them flat or clip them off using end-cutting pliers. You'll save measuring time by making a simple spacing jig as shown. This planter was finished with a clear exterior finish.

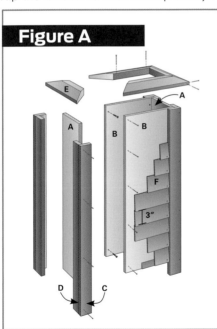

Figure A

A, A, B, B, E, F, D, C

3"

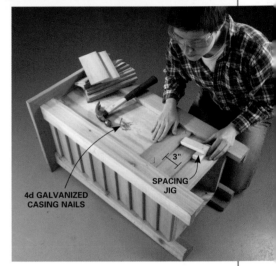

4d GALVANIZED CASING NAILS

SPACING JIG

3"

Cut a starter strip and lap siding to length and nail them to the plywood starting at the bottom and working up. Lap each row 1/2 in. over the siding below.

Materials List

1	4' x 8' x 3/4" CDX plywood
2	5/4x6 x 6' deck board
1	2x4 x 8' cedar or pine
36'	1/2" x 3-1/2" lap siding
	Water-resistant glue
	4d, 8d and 12d galvanized casing nails
	6d galvanized box nails
	1-1/4" deck screws
	Plastic planter (to fit 12" x 12" opening)

Cutting List

KEY	QTY.	SIZE & DESCRIPTION	KEY	QTY.	SIZE & DESCRIPTION
A	2	3/4" x 12" x 29" plywood ends	D	4	1" x 2" x 32" legs
B	2	3/4" x 13-1/2" x 29" plywood sides	E	4	1-1/2" x 3-1/2" x 19" beveled cap
C	4	1" x 3" x 32" legs	F	40	1/2" x 3-1/2" x 9-3/4" siding (cut to fit)

WHAT IT TAKES

Time: 1 day
Skill level: Beginner

Cedar shingle planter

Wood shingles are perfect for a rustic, natural-looking box. And finishing the planter is a snap if you use stain (we used a gray semi-transparent stain). The only drawback to shingles is that you may have to buy a whole bundle, many more than you'll need to side one planter.

The butt end of shingles is a little too thick for the proportions of this planter. So before cutting the shingles to their final length, trim off about 4 in. from the thick end (assuming your shingles are about 16 in. long). Then cut and install them as shown. Start with a double thickness of shingles on the first row. Then offset the joints by at least 1-1/2 in. from one row to the next. Also stagger the shingles up and down if you like the "shaggy" look. Nail the shingles to the plywood box with 3d galvanized box nails. Position the nails so the next row will cover them. The nails will stick through the inside of the box but won't interfere with the plastic liner.

Choosing a finish

Cedar shingles can be stained to extend their life, but they shouldn't be painted. Cedar shingles need to breathe. When the exterior surface is painted, the backs still absorb moisture, which "pushes" the paint off the shingles.

Cut 4 in. off the thick end of all 16-in. shingles to reduce their length to 12 in. Then cut them to fit and nail them to the plywood, starting at the bottom. Stagger the slots between shingles.

Figure B
Cedar shingle planter

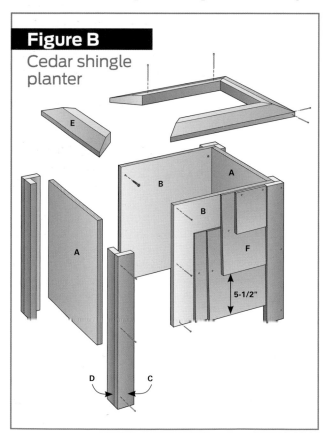

Materials List

1	16" x 62" x 3/4" CDX plywood
1	5/4x6 x 8' deck board
1	2x4 x 8' cedar or pine
1	Bundle of cedar shingles (50 or 60)
	Water-resistant glue
	8d and 12d galvanized casing nails
	3d and 6d galvanized box nails
	1-1/4" deck screws
	Plastic planter (to fit 13" x 13" opening)

Cutting List

KEY	QTY.	SIZE & DESCRIPTION
A	2	3/4" x 16" x 14-1/2" plywood ends
B	2	3/4" x 16" x 16" plywood sides
C	4	1" x 3" x 19" legs
D	4	1" x 2" x 19" legs
E	4	1-1/2" x 3-1/2" x 20" beveled cap
F	50-60	12" cedar shingles cut to fit

WHAT IT TAKES

Time: 1 day
Skill level: Beginner

Build a paver path

Pavers have been around since the Romans cut stones and placed them on a gravel bed to make incredibly durable roads. They can withstand heavy use. Modern versions are made from concrete, clay or stone. A paver path is a labor-intensive project that requires the rental of a heavy plate compactor (photo left) for proper installation. But the result is a permanent, tight-fitting, relatively smooth path that rivals solid concrete for durability.

Pavers are designed to lie in a tight pattern. Colors and patterns vary widely.

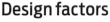

Plate compactor

Design factors

Best uses: All-around excellent material for paths, walks and even driveways, since paver construction can withstand heavy weight. They're highly decorative. You can choose from a variety of colors and patterns, creating anything from a formal English garden walk to an ancient-looking cobblestone path.

Versatility: Ideal for straight or curved paths. However, since pavers require a compact gravel base, changing the path later is a huge job. Use with caution around mature trees, so you don't damage the roots.

Longevity/maintenance: This type of path will last a lifetime. To avoid weeds, sweep off dirt so it doesn't accumulate in the joints. Every few years, sweep more sand into the joints to keep the pavers secure.

Drainage: Set the path to drain at 1/4 in. per foot to the side. Set the pavers slightly above the surrounding grade.

Slopes: Pavers can be laid on steep inclines (if you can walk up the incline, pavers can be laid on it), but don't use them for steps. Use stone, concrete or wood for the steps instead.

Concrete pavers

Antique clay paver

Materials

Concrete pavers are the most common and diverse, available in different colors and shapes. You can arrange each shape in a number of patterns. They have beveled edges for easier fitting and shoveling. Expect them to last 30 years or more. The color will fade slightly as they weather.

Clay pavers were commonly used for streets in the 1900s. Many versions are available today, from soft-textured molded styles to crisp edge types. Color retention and durability are excellent. Set them perfectly even; the edges on some types can chip. Be sure what you buy is a paver, not a house brick, which is softer and will deteriorate.

Stone pavers are the most expensive, at least twice the price of clay or concrete pavers. They're often tumbled to make them look old. They're incredibly hard and difficult to cut, but they're attractive and will last a lifetime.

You'll find the largest selection of all types of pavers at a landscape, brick or stone supplier. You can usually find concrete pavers at home centers as well.

Clay pavers

Granite paver

Key construction details

Setting pavers involves a lot of repetitious work and isn't a job for a novice. You first dig a pathway about 9 in. deep and fill and compact the base material (gravel that packs well) with a special plate compactor. Then you lay the edging, spread and level a bed of sand and drop in the pavers. You usually have to cut some pavers to fit with a saw and diamond blade. To finish, set the pavers with the plate compactor and then sweep sand into the joints.

Concrete pavers are cast in a wide variety of geometric shapes and colors. Most have rounded edges.

Clay pavers offer the traditional brick look. Most have crisp, square edges.

Stone pavers are cut from natural stone and are a uniform size. They often have rough faces.

Simple garden archway

Turn rustic materials into a flowering arch

Looking for a garden feature that's low cost and easy to assemble? Then this archway trellis is perfect. It's made from inexpensive steel "rebar" that you can find at any home center. Once the trellis is covered with climbing plants, the steel disappears and you have a dramatic entryway into your garden.

This design, about 7 ft. high and 6 ft. wide, is made of two 20-ft. lengths of rebar that you bend into arches. You then simply join the arches with rebar circles, lashing them together with wraps of copper wire. No welding needed—and there's no maintenance. The materials for this trellis cost less than $25. For comparison, a welded metal or high-end vinyl trellis costs several hundred dollars.

Here you'll learn how to create smooth bends in rebar and how to assemble the trellis. You'll need a few simple tools, including a conduit bender for tight curves and a hacksaw for cutting the bar to length. You may want to pick up an angle grinder and a metal-cutting blade for quicker rebar cuts. And don't forget to buy a pair of heavy leather gloves.

Allow a full day to build your first trellis. Once you've mastered the process, you should be able to build a second one in less than half a day. Rebar itself is relatively inexpensive: A 20-ft. length of 1/2-in. costs about $7 and 3/8-in. about $5. The main problem is getting your 20-ft. lengths home. Rebar is floppy, not stiff. One trick is to buy a 16-ft.-long 2x4, attach it to your roof rack and then lash the rebar to it. (Be sure to attach a red flag to each end of it.) Otherwise, delivery costs vary from $50 to more than $100.

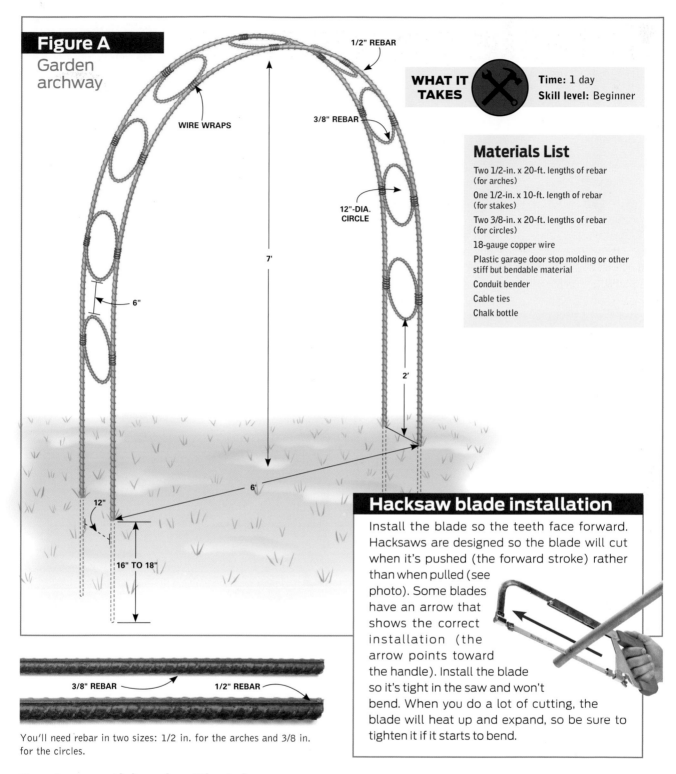

Figure A
Garden archway

1/2" REBAR

WIRE WRAPS

3/8" REBAR

12"-DIA. CIRCLE

7'

6"

2'

6'

12"

16" TO 18"

WHAT IT TAKES

Time: 1 day
Skill level: Beginner

Materials List

Two 1/2-in. x 20-ft. lengths of rebar (for arches)

One 1/2-in. x 10-ft. length of rebar (for stakes)

Two 3/8-in. x 20-ft. lengths of rebar (for circles)

18-gauge copper wire

Plastic garage door stop molding or other stiff but bendable material

Conduit bender

Cable ties

Chalk bottle

3/8" REBAR   1/2" REBAR

You'll need rebar in two sizes: 1/2 in. for the arches and 3/8 in. for the circles.

Hacksaw blade installation

Install the blade so the teeth face forward. Hacksaws are designed so the blade will cut when it's pushed (the forward stroke) rather than when pulled (see photo). Some blades have an arrow that shows the correct installation (the arrow points toward the handle). Install the blade so it's tight in the saw and won't bend. When you do a lot of cutting, the blade will heat up and expand, so be sure to tighten it if it starts to bend.

Create smooth bends with stakes

To create that swooping arch from the 1/2-in. rebar, make a simple bending jig on the ground. Cut the 10-ft. length of 1/2-in. rebar into ten 10-in.-long stakes (Photo 1). Drive one rebar stake into the ground and tie a 3-ft. string to it. When you pull the string taut, you create a compass and can mark a smooth arc with chalk (Photo 2). Space the other nine stakes evenly in a semicircle around the arc, driving them at least 5 in. deep (Photo 3).

The 3-ft. radius makes an arch that will span 6 ft. You can make it larger or slightly smaller if you want. But bending 1/2-in. rebar into a 2-ft. radius is difficult.

Rebar may kink when you bend it, so insert a cushion (a 9-ft. length of plastic garage door stop molding; sold at home centers) between the rebar and the stakes to soften the bend (Photo 4). You can use some other firm but flexible item, like vinyl siding or a strip of flexible hardboard to cushion the rebar as well.

Photo 4 shows how to bend the arches. Hold the rebar at the ends while you bend it to keep the arch smooth.

1 Cut 1/2-in. rebar into ten 10-in. stakes. Saw about two-thirds of the way through with a hacksaw, then snap off the stake.

2 Drive a stake and tie a string to it. Mark a 3-ft.-radius arc on the lawn using the string to guide the chalk bottle.

3 Space nine stakes evenly around the semicircle, and drive them down about 5 in. Mark the middle stake with a string.

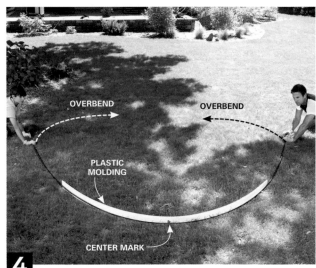

4 Lay plastic molding around the stakes. With a helper, center the rebar on the middle stake and push the ends around the semicircle.

Overbend it slightly; the ends will spring back a bit when you release them. Don't worry about that; the arches will form the correct radius when you set them in the ground.

Create circles with a conduit bender

Link the arches together with circles bent from the 3/8-in. rebar. Cut the rebar into 4-ft. lengths and bend them with a 1/2-in. conduit bender (available in the electrical department of any home center or hardware store). Work on a solid surface and simply fit one end of the rebar into the lip of the bender. Then form the curve by pulling the handle and pressing down on the tool with your foot (Photo 5). Shift the bender and continue the bend until you have a complete circle. The circle will have a 12-in. diameter. Cut off the extra rebar. Don't worry if the circles aren't perfect. Minor imperfections will be minimized when

you wire them to the arches, and hidden when your greenery grows.

Assemble the arches

Now find the ideal spot in your yard for the trellis and lay out the footprint (Photo 6). To keep it sturdy and stable, you have to sink each arch end about 18 in. into the ground. Measure up each leg and wrap tape at the 18-in. mark as a depth guide (Photo 7). With a helper, press the ends of the two arches into the ground. Drive a stake partway down to get started, or use a 3/4-in. steel pipe as a holder (see "Solution for hard soil," p. 69).

> **CAUTION**
> Call 811 or visit call811.com to locate underground lines before you dig.

Then add the 3/8-in. rebar circles. Position the first circle about 2 ft. up from the bottom of your arch. Any

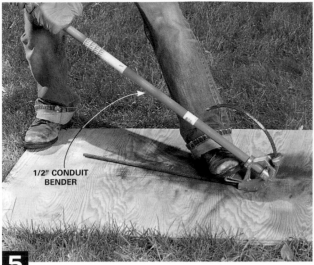

5 Bend the rebar into a circle with a conduit bender. Cut off the extra rebar. Repeat until you have nine circles.

1/2" CONDUIT BENDER

6 Position the anchor holes for the trellis 6 ft. apart and 12 in. between arches. Drive in stakes to start the holes, then pull them out.

CHALK

7 Position the trellis and push the ends 18 in. deep into the ground. Mark the depth with masking tape.

MASKING TAPE MARK

8 Position the circles between the arches with cable ties. Then tightly bind the circles to the arches with 2-ft. lengths of copper wire. Wire down as much of the side of the circle as you can to make the circle stable.

COPPER WIRE

CABLE TIE

lower and you may be inviting little feet to use the trellis as a makeshift ladder. Use cable ties to temporarily secure the circles in place, with the cut ends against one arch (Photo 8). Later you'll cover these sharp edges with the wire wrap. Space the remaining circles evenly around the arch. They'll be about 6 in. apart. The cable ties allow you to easily reposition the circles for the best appearance before you wire them into place.

To bind the circles, simply wrap the copper wire around the arch/circle joint. There is no special technique here. About 2 ft. of 18-gauge solid copper wire will do. Just keep the binding tight and extend it about 2 in. along the joint for good stiffness. Finally, tap the wire ends down flat to the rebar with a hammer.

Once you attach the circles to the arches, your trellis is ready to shepherd creeping vines upward, adding height and dimension to your outdoor space.

Solution for hard soil

If you have hard soil, you won't be able to push the arches directly into the ground. Instead, you'll have to plant the rebar arches in a pipe. Drive an 18-in. length of 3/4-in. galvanized pipe most of the way into the ground as shown. Pull out the pipe and poke the dirt from the inside of the pipe until it's open. Then push the 3/4-in. pipe back into the hole and drive it down until it's flush with the ground. Now, simply insert the arch ends in the pipe.

Container water gardens

Great ponds in small packages

Container gardens with aquatic plants create more mystery than plants potted in soil. They make you want to go outside and have a look. Plus, they're extremely low maintenance. Top them off with water before you go on vacation, and they're still bright and beautiful when you come home. And if you add a spouting ornament or water movement of any kind, the kids will love it even more than you do.

Container water gardens are inexpensive and easy to build, too. So here's how to get into the swim of things with a container water garden.

WHAT IT TAKES | **Time:** 2 hours
Skill level: Beginner

WATER TUBE CONNECTOR

MOUNTING SPIKE

CAT LITTER

PEA GRAVEL

1 Drill a small hole in the rim of the container to mount the spouting ornament. If you need to bend the support spike to level or position the spouter, grip it with two pairs of pliers so you don't crack the ornament.

2 Spread the soil of the lily or other deep-water plants in one half of the container, then add cat litter to create a level floor.

What you need

For a basic garden, you need at least an 18- to 20-in. plastic container that's 7 to 8 in. deep, a small submersible pump, a spouting ornament, plants, clear vinyl tubing, clean cat litter, pea gravel or small pebbles and a nylon stocking. Most items are readily available at larger garden centers or online.

How to do it

The photos show you how. Here are a few additional tips:

- The floor is two-tiered to allow for different types of plants; the lilies planted on the deep side have stems that float upward and extend horizontally, while the "marginal" plants—those that grow upright and favor shallower water—stand on the higher side. The partition that separates the two sides can be made from stone, bricks or other heavy material.
- Pea gravel both beautifies your water garden and acts as a lid over the unpotted soil so it can't circulate and darken the water. Rinse the pea gravel before adding it to the container.
- For extra protection, place the pump in a nylon stocking before putting it in the cup, then stuff the extra nylon over the pump. This filtering is crucial; otherwise pebbles and cat litter will be drawn into the pump and clog it. A well-filtered pump will run for months; a clogged pump must be dug up, which fouls the water.
- Small submersible pumps have adjustable pressure, so before burying the pump, place it in a bucket of water, plug it in and adjust the pressure of the jet of water coming out of the spouter.
- Fill a couple of buckets with tap water, then let them sit for a day or two to allow chlorine to evaporate and water temperature to moderate. Pour the water in gradually—it should be as clear as a mountain stream.
- Aquatic plants thrive on direct sunlight, so a bright sunny spot is ideal. If possible, position the container near an electrical outlet for the pump.

Project at a glance

Skill level: beginner
Special tools: drill
Approximate cost:
$50-$100

Plan smart

Wind can wreak havoc with tall plants by pushing the containers off their pedestals. Finding a wind-free space helps solve this problem and ensures the fountain arc from the spouting ornament looks and sounds the way you want it to.

MARGINAL
PLANTS

FLAGSTONE
PARTITION

PLASTIC
COVER

3 Add a partition to divide the container into halves. Plant the shallow-growing marginal plants and spread more cat litter over the soil. On the low side, nestle a plastic cup for the pump in the cat litter, keeping it covered with plastic to prevent gravel from falling in.

LOWER
SIDE

PEA
GRAVEL

4 Spread pea gravel over the cat litter. Keep the floor on the lily side lower to allow the lily stems room to extend upward when you add water.

Care, maintenance and something fishy

Taking care of water gardens is a breeze. Top them off as water evaporates and scoop off the occasional dead leaf or bit of algae.

Plants maintain water clarity by absorbing decaying matter through their roots as food. But if the water starts looking gunky, remove the plants, rinse the container and refill.

For any plants needing a boost, press a fertilizer pellet into the potting soil. You can also add a mosquito killer (sold at garden centers) a couple times in the summer to kill mosquito larvae without posing harm to people or pets. Smaller containers will only need a small piece.

For a small container, plant a dwarf lily so the pads don't completely cover the surface as they grow. For larger water gardens, you can add a floating plant like water hyacinth, duckweed or water lettuce.

A dish-style garden is too small for goldfish, but larger containers, like whiskey barrels or larger terra-cotta pots, are ideal. (Note: Water in metal containers usually gets too warm for fish.) Fish help keep the garden clean by eating algae, decaying plant material and mosquito larvae. Make certain to read up on fish so you give them the proper care and learn how they will impact your garden.

Handy Hints

You can overwinter hardy water lilies by wrapping them in a damp towel and storing them in a cool basement or garage corner. Other plants are relatively inexpensive and grow rapidly, so in cold climates, buy them anew each year and treat as annuals.

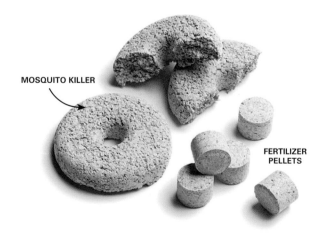

MOSQUITO KILLER

FERTILIZER
PELLETS

SECTION OF 1/2" TUBING

3/8" TUBING

SUCTION CUPS

5 Connect the pump to the spouter with vinyl tubing. Use a transition piece of 1/2-in. tubing if necessary to connect the 3/8-in. tube to the pump. Press the pump into the cup so that the suction cups anchor it to the bottom.

NYLON FILTER

6 Cover the pump with a nylon stocking filter to keep gravel from clogging the pump, and then cover the pump with pea gravel.

The Super-Simple Approach

If you want an instant water garden, simply slip a plastic barrel liner into a decorative wooden barrel, set some pavers of various heights in place to act as pedestals and then perch a few potted aquatic plants on top. Just make sure to position the plants at the depth indicated on the plant tag or information sheet. The only drawback to this approach is that the container won't look as natural close up—you can see the plastic pots below the surface. You can even add a spouter to the barrel; the pump can simply sit on a pedestal without a cup.

If you can't find a plastic barrel liner, you can make a watertight terra cotta container by plugging the drain hole with plumber's epoxy (left) and applying two coats of polyurethane.

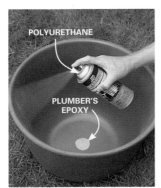

POLYURETHANE

PLUMBER'S EPOXY

LINER

PAVER PEDESTALS

Pre-season snow blower maintenance

Get your snow blower ready for action by installing a new spark plug, changing the oil and checking the condition of the belts. Replace the belts if you see cracks, fraying or glazing or notice that chunks are missing.

Next, sand any rusted areas and repaint. Once the paint cures, apply a high-quality polymeric car wax (available from any auto parts store) to all painted surfaces. The wax will shed the snow and water and protect the paint. And wax the inside of the chute to help prevent clogs.

Then consult your owner's manual to find the lubrication points and the recommended lube. If the type of lube isn't listed, here's some general guidance: Use motor oil on metal linkage joints, gears and cables, but dry PTFE lube on plastic parts (knobs, gears and chute). Spray the auger, second-stage impeller and chute with silicone spray to prevent snow from sticking.

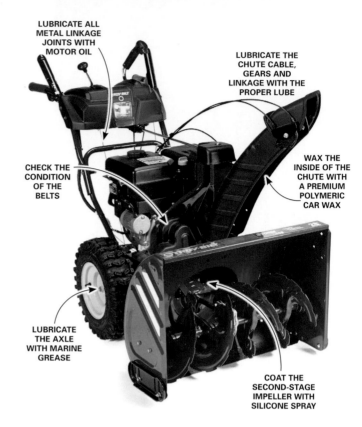

LUBRICATE ALL METAL LINKAGE JOINTS WITH MOTOR OIL

LUBRICATE THE CHUTE CABLE, GEARS AND LINKAGE WITH THE PROPER LUBE

CHECK THE CONDITION OF THE BELTS

WAX THE INSIDE OF THE CHUTE WITH A PREMIUM POLYMERIC CAR WAX

LUBRICATE THE AXLE WITH MARINE GREASE

COAT THE SECOND-STAGE IMPELLER WITH SILICONE SPRAY

Prevent major auger damage

The drive shaft applies torque to the shear pin, which then applies it to the auger. However, if the auger rusts to the drive shaft, they'll become one and the shear pin will never break. If that happens, the auger clog can cause major damage to the machine. Lubricate the drive shaft to prevent it from rusting to the auger.

Lube and spin: Remove shear pins and lubricate the drive shaft with lubricating oil.

Then spin the auger to spread the oil along the length of the shaft. Reinstall shear pins.

Buy parts before you need them

Belts and shear pins always break on a Sunday night in the middle of a blizzard. So buy replacement parts at the start of the season when everyone has them in stock. If you break a shear pin and try to improvise using the wrong shear pin—or worse yet, an ordinary bolt—you risk major damage that can easily cost you $200. A set of belts and a few extra shear pins will cost about $25. Also make sure you have the right size of wrenches and sockets and the correct size pin punch to drive out the broken pin. Then assemble a parts and tool kit.

NEW SHEAR PINS

PIN PUNCH

REPLACEMENT BELTS

Make a gravel path

Less costly than brick or slate, more natural looking than concrete, gravel makes a fine path for formal and informal gardens alike. Best of all, a gravel path is also easier to make.

- Dig the path to a depth of at least 6 in.
- Edge the path with vinyl or steel edging and stake it in place.
- Lay down landscape fabric to suppress weeds.
- Cover the fabric with 3 in. of sand, then 3 in. of 3/8-in. crushed limestone or washed pea gravel. You'll find that smaller stones like this make a path that's denser, more attractive and weed resistant, as well as easier to walk on.

CRUSHED WASHED GRAVEL

CRUSHED LIMESTONE

PEA ROCK

Perfect path materials

Gravel is available in many sizes and colors. Ask for gravel that compacts well. It'll typically have stones ranging in size from 3/4 in. down to a powder. Smaller stones (3/8 in.) are the most comfortable underfoot. Larger (3/4 in.) stones stay put better during rainstorms.

Buy your gravel from a landscape supplier or directly from a quarry.

WHAT IT TAKES

Time: 1 day
Skill level: Beginner

Self-watering planter

Build a raised planting bed and have tonight's salad at your fingertips!

Growing veggies during high summer means daily watering, which becomes a problem when you go away for vacation. To keep plants healthy, build "self-watering" veggie planters that can be left for weeks without watering. The planter boxes look great, plus they keep rabbits and other critters from munching on your greens. In this article, we'll show you how to build one for yourself. The secret is in the perforated drain pipe.

1/2" VINYL DRAIN TUBE

PERFORATED DRAIN PIPE WITH FABRIC SLEEVE

Top 8 reasons to build this planter:

1. It saves your back and knees.
2. You'll have fewer weeds.
3. It waters your plants while you're away.
4. It saves water.
5. You'll have fresh veggies steps from your back door.
6. It's easy to create the perfect soil.
7. It protects your veggies from hungry critters.
8. It's a handsome addition to your patio.

Self-watering planters are sometimes called "sub-irrigated planters" or SIPs, because your plants get to "sip" water whenever they want. Our version uses inexpensive perforated drain pipe with a fabric sleeve in the bottom of the planter. Once you fill the drain pipe reservoirs, they allow air to circulate and water to wick up to your plants' roots whenever they need it.

When plants are watered from below, the roots stay consistently moist, there's less evaporation and you don't need to water as much. The vinyl tubing allows any overflow water to drain. There are many commercial self-watering planters available at garden centers and online. But you can easily make your own.

Build your planting box

Photos 1 – 6 show you how to build a handsome wood planter box. The total cost of this 3 x 6-ft. cedar planter was about $350. If you use treated wood, the price would drop to about $250. We used a thick EPDM pond liner, which cost $120. You can buy thinner versions at home centers for about $35. To give the box a nice finished look, we routed the boards and sanded the faces and cap. We left the cedar unfinished, but you could seal yours. After we built the basic box, we moved the planter to its final position and then added the self-watering system, soil

1 **Screw the box ends together.** Pick the straightest 2x2s for the corner cleats. Align the parts with the corner of your work-table to keep the assembly square.

2 **Construct the box sides.** Straighten bowed boards with a clamp. The top boards need to be straight so the cap will go on straight and tight.

3 **Screw the box together.** Clamp the edges together and press firmly with the other hand when screwing each plank so everything comes together tightly.

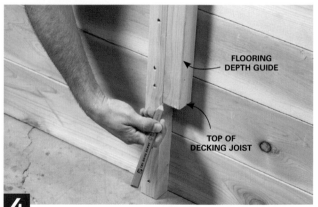

4 **Mark for the decking joists.** Determine the floor depth (see "Building tips" below), and cut a block that length to mark the locations of the horizontal cleats and joists.

Building tips

- When assembling the box ends (Photo 1) and sides (Photo 2), leave gaps between the planks to allow for expansion and contraction. Use 1/16-in. washers as spacers.
- To determine where to put your planter floor (Photo 4), add together your soil depth, the flooring thickness and the height of the drain pipe and add an inch to that so the soil level will sit an inch below the top of the box.
- For greater strength, use 2x2 horizontal cleats (33 in. long for our planter) for each end and 2x4s for the center two joists.
- Don't miter the top cap—miter joints open with changes in humidity. Butt joints will look neater than miter joints over time.
- Cut the perforated drain pipe into 6-ft. lengths

and lay them in rows across the bottom of the planter. Wedging them in place against the sides will prevent potting mix from getting into the pipes, so you don't need to cap the ends.
- Wedge the CPVC fill tube tightly into the top of the drain pipe. It should be long enough to poke out of the top of your soil once your container is planted (Photo 7). You only need one fill tube in the planter because the water will flow through the perforations of the pipe section with the fill tube and then into surrounding soilless potting mix and through the perforations of all the other drain pipes.
- You can buy perforated drain pipe with an attached sleeve at home centers and land-scape centers.

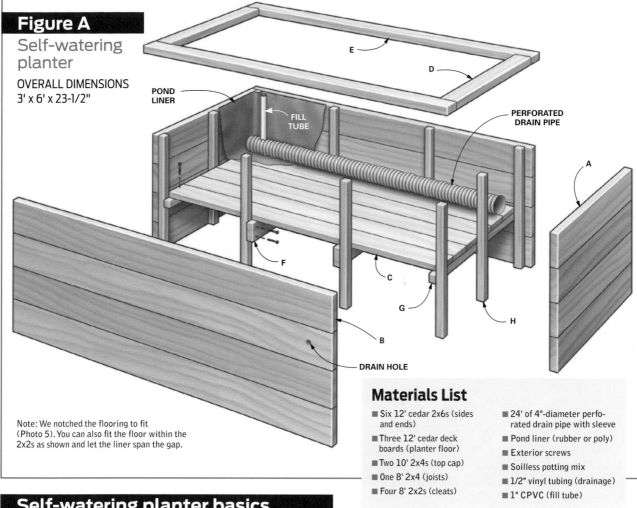

Figure A
Self-watering planter

OVERALL DIMENSIONS
3' x 6' x 23-1/2"

POND LINER

FILL TUBE

PERFORATED DRAIN PIPE

E

D

A

F

C

G

H

B

DRAIN HOLE

Note: We notched the flooring to fit (Photo 5). You can also fit the floor within the 2x2s as shown and let the liner span the gap.

Materials List

- Six 12' cedar 2x6s (sides and ends)
- Three 12' cedar deck boards (planter floor)
- Two 10' 2x4s (top cap)
- One 8' 2x4 (joists)
- Four 8' 2x2s (cleats)
- 24' of 4"-diameter perforated drain pipe with sleeve
- Pond liner (rubber or poly)
- Exterior screws
- Soilless potting mix
- 1/2" vinyl tubing (drainage)
- 1" CPVC (fill tube)

Cutting List

The Cutting List gives finished lengths for the top, front, sides, cleats and bottom. You can cut these to the exact width and length listed and nail them together. The lengths listed for the 3/4-in. x 1-in. bands and the 3/4-in. cove moldings are oversized. You'll mark these pieces in place for an exact fit (Photo 1).

KEY	QTY.	SIZE & DESCRIPTION
A	8	1-1/2" x 5-1/2" x 33" (ends)
B	8	1-1/2" x 5-1/2" x 72" (sides)
C	6	1" x 5-1/2" (floor; cut to fit)
D	2	1-1/2" x 3-1/2" x 30" (end cap)
E	2	1-1/2" x 3-1/2" x 73" (side cap)
F	2	1-1/2" x 3-1/2" x 33" (joists)
G	2	1-1/2" x 1-1/2" x 33" (horizontal cleats)
H	10	1-1/2" x 1-1/2" x 22" (vertical cleats)

Self-watering planter basics

- Choose a spot that gets at least six hours of sun. If your planter is against a wall, you can get by with less sun because of the reflected heat.
- A 4-ft.-wide planter is ideal for harvesting from both sides. Keep it to 3 ft. wide if you're placing your planter against a wall or fence.
- Line your planter with a "fish-safe" rubber membrane. It will prolong the life of the wood without leaching chemicals into the soil (and your food). You can buy fish-safe pond liners in different thicknesses and materials at home centers, garden centers and online retailers.
- Don't use garden soil or a heavy potting soil in your raised garden. Use a light, fluffy "soilless" blend that will retain moisture without compacting or becoming waterlogged. You can also buy potting soil specifically formulated for self-watering planters.
- Mulch your containers to keep weeds down and to slow evaporation.
- For more great ideas for building sub-irrigated planters (SIPs), search for the term online.

Good choices for containers

Vegetables and Herbs	Soil Depth
Chives, lettuce, radishes, salad greens, basil and coriander	4 – 5 in.
Bush beans, garlic, onions, Asian greens, peas, mint and thyme	6 – 7 in.
Pole beans, carrots, chard, cucumbers, fennel, leeks, peppers, spinach, parsley and rosemary	8 – 9 in.
Beets, broccoli, potatoes, tomatoes, summer squash and dill	10 – 12 in.

and plants. Even without the soil and plants, this planter is heavy!

Photos 7 and 8 show you how to construct the self-watering system. Once you're ready to plant, add a soilless mix to just below the top of the planter.

Once your plants are in, fill the drain pipe reservoirs through the fill tube until water runs out the drainage hole (this can take a while). The water will slowly wick out of the perforated pipes into the potting mix packed around it and eventually up into the potting mix and plant roots above.

You'll have to experiment to see how long your planter will stay moist. Fill the drain pipes whenever the soil feels dry 2 or 3 in. down. When we set ours up, we filled the drain pipes and gave the plants an initial surface watering and then mulched around them. After that, and despite a record hot summer, we refilled the pipes only three times over the summer and we had herbs and greens growing until the first frost!

5 **Attach the joists and lay the floor.** Screw the horizontal end cleats in place first and then the center joists. Notch your deck boards to fit around the vertical supports.

2x2 HORIZONTAL CLEAT

2x4 JOISTS

6 **Staple the rubber membrane in place.** Fold the pond liner at the corners and staple it around the perimeter. Trim the excess.

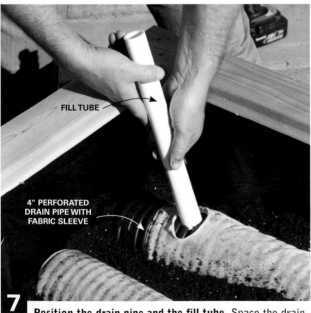

FILL TUBE

4" PERFORATED DRAIN PIPE WITH FABRIC SLEEVE

7 **Position the drain pipe and the fill tube.** Space the drain pipes evenly along the deck floor, wedging the ends tightly against the short sides of the planter. Pack potting mix around the pipes to keep them straight. Stick a fill tube in the top end of one of the outside drain pipes.

1/2" VINYL TUBE

8 **Drill a drain hole and fit the tubing.** In the end of the planter opposite your fill tube, drill a drainage hole just above the height of the pipe. Run vinyl tubing from the drain pipe to the drainage hole.

Rebar plant cage

3/8" REBAR

1/2" IRON PIPE

WIRE LOOP

HOOP

BENT UPRIGHT

16-GAUGE WIRE

HACKSAW

WHAT IT TAKES

Time: 2 hours
Skill level: Beginner

Covered with vines, this rustic metal plant cage makes an attractive addition to your flower garden. In the vegetable patch, it's a great support for peppers or tomatoes. It's built from inexpensive concrete reinforcing steel (rebar) connected by twisted wire.

You'll need three 10-ft. lengths of 3/8-in. (No. 3) rebar (you'll have a little extra) and about 20 ft. of 16- or 18-gauge wire. You'll find 3/8-in. rebar at home centers. Ask the supplier to cut standard 20-ft. lengths in half to make it easier to haul.

1 Bend 10-ft. lengths of 3/8-in. rebar around a 5-gallon bucket to form two arches as shown. Drill two holes in the side of the bucket and loop a wire through the holes and around the rebar to hold it in place while you do the bending. Slip a 3-ft. length of 1/2-in. pipe over the rebar for better leverage and control. Use the same technique for bending the hoops, but wrap the rebar completely around the bucket to form a circle. Then cut the straight section off with a hacksaw, leaving the hoop and a few inches of overlap. Wrap and twist-tie wire around the overlap to form the two hoops.

2 Stack the two hoops on the ground. Poke the ends of the two arches a few inches into the ground inside the hoops. Twist a 12-in. length of wire around the intersection of the two arches to secure them. Cut off the extra wire. Then slide the first loop up to about 16 in. from the top and wire it in place. Stand back and eyeball the hoop to make sure it's level and the uprights are evenly spaced before you tighten the tie wires. Repeat this process for the second hoop, leaving about 16 in. between hoops.

HOOPS CONNECTED

TWISTED WIRE

Low-upkeep mailbox

The strength of wood and the convenience of PVC!

WHAT IT TAKES

Time: 1 day
Skill level: Intermediate

If your old wooden mailbox is falling apart—or if it was run over by your teenage driver—this low-maintenance mailbox made from treated wood and PVC is the perfect replacement.

All the materials are available at any home center. The PVC post sleeves can be a little tricky to work with, but PVC boards are easy to cut and fasten with regular woodworking tools. And PVC doesn't tear out, split or splinter.

The whole project costs under $120. Building it takes about a day, including shopping and digging the post hole.

Start with a trip to the post office

Don't assume the dimensions used here will work for you. The height, distance from the curb and newspaper box requirements may be different in your area. The dimensions for this box are based on a pamphlet from the local post office. The USPS recommends that a post be buried no more than 24 in. It's safer if the post gives way if someone runs into it.

Cutting the parts

A 6-ft. fence post sleeve leaves virtually no extra length for cutting mistakes. Start your 45-degree cut as close to the end as possible; a 20-in. angle bracket will leave you a 52-in. post sleeve. Cut into the sleeve slowly; thinner plastic can shatter if you cut too aggressively, especially when it's cold. After cutting the angle bracket sleeve, use it as a template to mark the wood angle bracket. Once again, start your cut as close to the end as possible. An 8-ft. post with 20 in. cut off will leave you with 2 ft. of post to bury in the ground.

The two newspaper box sides (J) only need to be cut to length, but don't assume the factory ends are square—they're usually not. Trim just as much as necessary to make a true 90-degree end. After cutting the top (H) and bottom (G) to length, you'll need to cut them to width. Start by removing 1/4 in. from one side of each board to remove the rounded edges. The leftover scrap from the top should be about 1-1/8 in. wide. Save that piece to make the mailbox base.

Any circle with an 8- to 9-in. diameter will work as a template to mark the curves on the sides (Figure B). Once all the curves are cut, clamp the two sides together and sand the curves smooth so the pieces are identical.

The mailbox we used required a 17-1/2-in. x 6-1/8-in. base. Your mailbox might be different. The total length of the base is not the same as the length of the mailbox—it has to be about 1 in. shorter to allow the door to open. Cement the scraps (E and F) together to form a base board that fits your mailbox.

Cut kerfs in the bottom of the newspaper box (G) to allow water to drain. Set your table saw blade at a height of 1/4 in. and set your fence 1/2 in. from the blade. Run the board through, then flip it around and do the same on the other side. Then run both sides of the board through at 1 in. and then again at 1-1/2 in. The middle kerf should be centered at 2 in., but you may want to double-check and line the last kerf up manually. Practice on a sacrificial board.

Materials List

ITEM	QTY.
Mailbox	1
8' x 4x4 treated post	1
6' x 4x4 PVC/vinyl fence post sleeve	1
10' x 1x6 PVC trim	1
Vinyl fence post cap	1
Tube of PVC-vinyl-fence cement	1
Tube of white exterior-grade silicone	1
Box of 1-5/8" screws approved for treated lumber	1
Box of 3" screws approved for treated lumber	1
White hinged screw cover	4
Black hinged screw cover	4

Cutting List

KEY	QTY.	SIZE & DESCRIPTION
A	1	52" x 4" x 4" post sleeve
B	1	20" x 4" x 4" angle bracket sleeve
C	1	76" x 3-1/2" x 3-1/2" wood post
D	1	20" (long side) x 4" x 4" wood angle bracket
E	1	17-1/2" x 3/4" x 1-1/8" mailbox base
F	1	17-1/2" x 3/4" x 5" mailbox base (glue to part E)
G	1	14" x 3/4" x 4" newspaper box bottom (with kerf cuts)
H	1	20" x 3/4" x 4" newspaper box top
J	2	30" x 3/4" x 5-1/2" newspaper box sides

1 **Cut the side curves.** A dull blade actually works better than a sharp blade, which tends to grab and shake the PVC as it cuts. Cut one side of the newspaper box, then use it as a template to mark the other side.

DULL WOOD BLADE

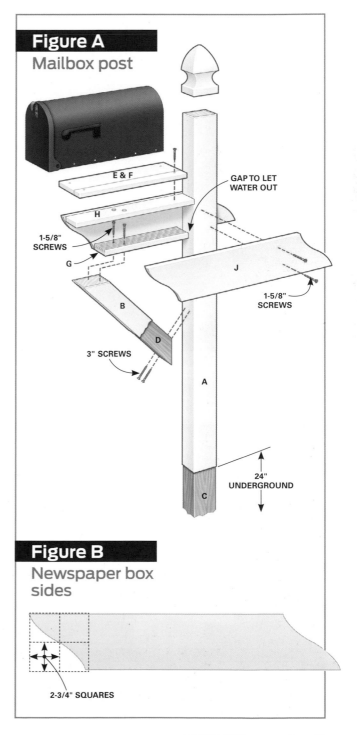

Figure A
Mailbox post

E & F

H

1-5/8" SCREWS

G

B

D

3" SCREWS

GAP TO LET WATER OUT

J

1-5/8" SCREWS

A

24" UNDERGROUND

C

Figure B
Newspaper box sides

2-3/4" SQUARES

Assemble the newspaper box

Use PVC-vinyl-fence cement to assemble the newspaper box. The cement is a little runny, so be prepared to wipe off the excess after clamping.

Clamp the box together, bottom side up. Hold both the top (H) and the bottom (G) out flush with the curves on the front of the sides (J), as shown in Photo 2. The bottom is shorter than the top at the back of the box. This gap allows water to escape.

Putting it all together

If your 4x4 post is twisted on one end, use the straight portion above ground. Slide the PVC sleeve over the post, leaving it flush at the top. Attach the wood angle bracket. Slide on the angle bracket sleeve (Photo 3).

Once the newspaper box is in place, clamp a framing square onto the post to ensure a true 90 degrees (Photo 4). Don't worry about splitting the small areas between the kerfs—PVC is much more forgiving than wood.

Screw the mailbox base to the newspaper box flush with the front edge of the box. Use 1-5/8-in. screws, and be sure to screw down into the sides or your screws will poke through into the box. Attach the mailbox to the base. Slide it all the way forward to allow room for the door to open (Photo 5).

Apply the cement to the cap, not the post—it's less messy. We used a pretty basic fence post cap, but feel free to decorate your post with a fancier cap, or one with a built-in solar light.

There will be a little play in the vinyl angle bracket sleeve. Use a putty knife to slip a bit of cement underneath each end of the sleeve in order to seal it to the newspaper box and post. Caulk both sides of the angle bracket with white exterior-grade caulk. Silicone is the easiest to work with. You're done!

2 **Assemble the box, bottom side up.** Dry-fit the entire newspaper box before you apply any cement. Cut a couple of 4-in. blocks to hold the bottom (G) at the right height. Tape along the joints to catch excess cement. Work fast—the cement won't wait.

3 **Screw on the wood angle bracket.** Most post sleeves aren't perfectly square, but slightly rectangular with one side a hair wider than the other. Attach the bracket to the narrow side. The newspaper box will slide on easier that way.

4 **Fasten the newspaper box.** Bore two 3/4-in. access holes in the top of the box. You will need a magnetic bit holder at least 4 in. long to reach the screws that attach the box to the angle bracket.

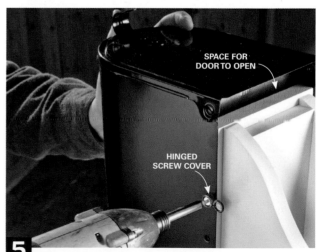

5 **Mount the mailbox.** Leave a gap under the mailbox door so it can open without binding against the base (E). Hinged screw covers snap shut and hide the screw heads for a clean look.

Summer lounge chair

WHAT IT TAKES

Time: 1 day
Skill level: Intermediate

Most wooden outdoor chairs can get uncomfortable in a half hour. This one is designed so you can settle in and knock off a few magazines or even catch a snooze. The cushion adds an extra bit of staying power, and the slats will help keep you cool. And you'll like the built-in tray on the back for holding your snack and phone.

Every detail of this chair is engineered for simplicity of construction, starting with the use of standard-width lumber for the parts.

While a power miter box is ideal for cutting the parts to length, you could easily use a circular saw or even a jigsaw for all the cuts. You'll also need a drill/driver and spring clamps for assembly.

These chairs are pine, but you could choose fir, cedar, treated pine or any other wood that can handle the outdoors. The pine for each chair cost about $35. Order the cushion online, or use any chair cushion about 18 to 20 in. square.

Select the best boards

You'll need only 1x3s (3/4 in. x 2-1/2 in.) and 1x4s (3/4 in. x 3-1/2 in.) for this project. Choose wood that either is knot free or has only small, tight knots. Look for straight boards, but they don't have to be perfect because you'll cut them into shorter lengths. If you can't find good 1x3s, buy 1x6s and rip 2-1/2-in.-wide pieces from them. You can ask the lumberyard to do it if you don't have access to a table saw.

Assemble the chair seat and back

Do all your assembly work on a flat benchtop or floor area in your garage or shop. Begin the process by cutting the seat box parts. It's easier to give the parts a quick sanding at this point than to sand the project after assembly. Then drill pilot and countersink holes and assemble the box with 1-5/8-in. deck screws. (See Photo 1 and Figure A.) A No. 8 pilot/countersink bit lets you quickly predrill and countersink in one step. Next cut the seat supports (C) using a miter saw or an angle guide to cut the 75-degree angle. An adjustable quick square (sold at home centers and hardware stores) works great as a cutting guide (Photo 2). Spread an exterior glue and screw the supports to the sides of the box with 1-1/4-in. galvanized screws (Photo 3).

Cut the seat back sides (E) and the seat top (B) and then glue and screw these pieces together with 1-5/8-in. deck screws. Next, glue and screw the back supports (D) to the seat back sides, making sure the supports extend 3-1/2 in. beyond the ends of the sides.

With the seat box assembly lying flat, insert the back assembly and align the back supports (D) directly behind the seat supports (C) and secure them with clamps (Photo 4). Drill two 1/4-in. holes through each seat box side and through the back supports. Insert 1/4-in. x 2-in. carriage bolts, add a washer and tighten the nuts with a wrench.

Bolt the legs to the chair

Mark the legs and seat frame with an adjustable square set at 10 degrees. Then draw a 10-degree line on the sides of the seat frame, 2-1/2 in. from the front and back (Figure B), to mark the leg positions. Also mark on the back edge of the rear legs at 6-3/4 in. and on the back edge of the front legs at 10-3/4 in. (Figure B).

1 Cut the sides (A) and ends (B) for the seat box. Drill pilot and countersink holes and screw the box together with 1-5/8-in. deck screws.

Figure A
Lounge chair details

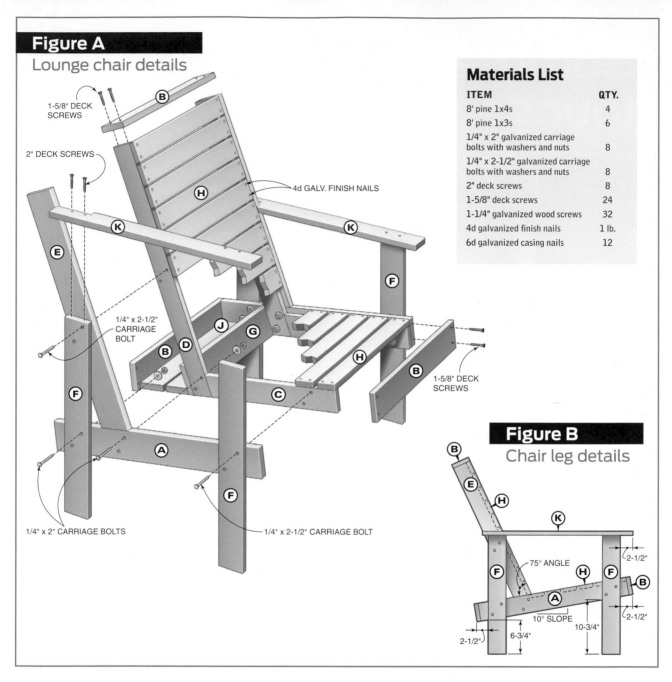

1-5/8" DECK SCREWS

2" DECK SCREWS

4d GALV. FINISH NAILS

1/4" x 2-1/2" CARRIAGE BOLT

1/4" x 2" CARRIAGE BOLTS

1/4" x 2-1/2" CARRIAGE BOLT

1-5/8" DECK SCREWS

Materials List

ITEM	QTY.
8' pine 1x4s	4
8' pine 1x3s	6
1/4" x 2" galvanized carriage bolts with washers and nuts	8
1/4" x 2-1/2" galvanized carriage bolts with washers and nuts	8
2" deck screws	8
1-5/8" deck screws	24
1-1/4" galvanized wood screws	32
4d galvanized finish nails	1 lb.
6d galvanized casing nails	12

Figure B
Chair leg details

75° ANGLE

10° SLOPE

2-1/2"

2-1/2"

2-1/2"

6-3/4"

10-3/4"

Cutting List

KEY	QTY.	SIZE & DESCRIPTION
A	2	3/4" x 3-1/2" x 30" seat box sides
B	3	3/4" x 3-1/2" x 21-1/2" seat top and box ends
C	2	3/4" x 2-1/2" x 19-1/2" seat supports (measure to long point of 75° angle)
D	2	3/4" x 2-1/2" x 32-9/16" back supports (measure to long point of 75° angle)
E	2	3/4" x 3-1/2" x 29-1/8" seat back sides (measure to long point of 75° angle)
F	4	3/4" x 3-1/2" x 23-1/2" legs
G	1	3/4" x 3-1/2" x 20" back seat brace
H	17	3/4" x 2-1/2" x 20" seat and back slats
J	2	3/4" x 3-1/2" x 20" storage tray slats
K	2	3/4" x 2-1/2" x 30" arms

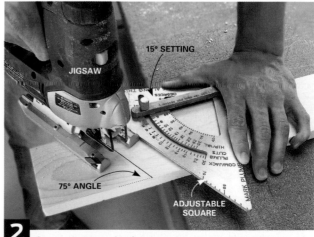

15° SETTING

JIGSAW

75° ANGLE

ADJUSTABLE SQUARE

2 Cut accurate angles for the seat supports (C), using an adjustable angle guide as a straightedge to guide your jigsaw or circular saw.

3 Glue and screw the seat supports (C) to the sides of the seat box (A) with 1-1/4-in. galvanized screws. Wipe off excess glue that squeezes out.

4 Cut, drill and assemble the parts for the back (Figure A). Then clamp the back to the seat frame, drill 1/4-in. holes and install the carriage bolts.

5 Position the legs and clamp them to the frame using Figure B as a guide. Drill and fasten them with carriage bolts. Nail the rear storage tray slats to the sides.

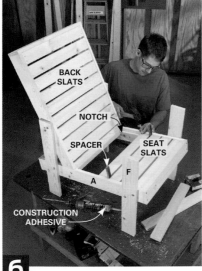

6 Cut the seat and back slats to length. Glue and nail them with 4d galvanized finish nails. Use two spacers to ensure consistent gaps.

7 Notch the arms to fit around the seat back frame. Then predrill and fasten the arms to the front and rear legs with 2-in. deck screws.

8 Soak the legs overnight in a wood preservative or an oil-based deck stain to slow water absorption. Once the legs are dry, prime and paint.

Align the marks on the legs and the seat frame and clamp the parts into place (Photo 5). Be sure the front and back legs are parallel and that both legs are square to the work surface. Clamp the legs to the seat frame and the back. Drill 1/4-in. holes and bolt the legs to the seat and back. Cut the two slats (J) for the rear shelf and the back seat brace (G) and nail them to the sides with 6d galvanized casing nails.

Nail the seat and back slats

Cut the slats (H) for the seat and back. Starting at the top of the seat back, fasten the slats with glue and 4d (1-1/2-in.) galvanized finish nails. The 1x3s used here were 2-5/8 in. wide and spaced every 3/8 in. If your 1x3s are narrower, adjust the spacing or add another slat. You'll

probably have to notch the lowest slat on the back to fit around the seat supports (Photo 6).

Now glue and nail the seat slats to the seat supports, starting at the front. Adjust the spacing to get a good fit.

To complete the chair, cut the arms and hold each on top of the legs so it overhangs the corresponding front leg 2-1/2 in. Then mark the back of the arm and notch it 3/4 in. with your jigsaw so it fits tightly against the side of the seat back (Photo 7). Fasten the arms so the outer sides overhang the legs by 1 in.

No matter what finish you choose, be sure to soak the legs in a preservative or deck stain to keep water from wicking up and ruining the finish or causing rot (Photo 8). If you paint, use an oil-based primer followed by two topcoats of a high-quality gloss or semigloss acrylic paint.

Coat hooks for DIYers

Distinctive hooks, DIY style

Looking for a present for a DIYer (or yourself)? Here's a gallery of creative coat hook ideas to spark your imagination.

Hitch pins

Antique doorknobs

Mason's trowels

SCREW FROM THE BACK

Hammers make great hooks

Valves & pipes

DADO AND EPOXY

C-clamps

Screws & bolts

HOT

COLD

Faucet handles

Cleats

THREADED ROD IN ANGLED HOLE

Hand screw clamps

Gutter deck planter

WHAT IT TAKES

Time: 1 hour
Skill level: Beginner

This lightweight, durable and attractive deck planter is made from a vinyl gutter, two fascia support brackets and two end caps. It's a snap to make. Glue one of the end caps in place and drill holes in the bottom of the gutter so the water can drain (Photo 1). Slide two fascia support brackets onto the gutter (Photo 2) and glue the other end cap into place. If you want a longer planter, be sure to add extra brackets spaced about every 2 ft.—dirt is heavy.

To prevent the soil from slipping through the drainage holes, line the gutter with newspaper or put shards of old broken clay pots along the bottom.

Shallow planters like these have a tendency to dry out. To cut your watering chore in half, mix water-absorbing polymer gel crystals (available at garden centers) with your potting mix. Or buy bags of soilless potting mix with the polymer crystals already added.

If you want a color other than white, use a spray paint formulated for plastic. Screw the planter to your deck rail (Photo 3), fill it with potting mix and add your plants. Enjoy!

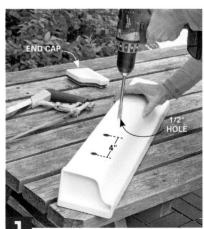

1 Cut a 2-ft. length of vinyl gutter and glue one of the end caps into place with kitchen and bath adhesive caulk. Drill 1/2-in. drainage holes every 4 in. along the bottom of the gutter.

2 Slide both fascia support brackets onto the gutter and glue the other end cap into place.

3 Screw the planter to the deck rail through the fascia support brackets using galvanized screws.

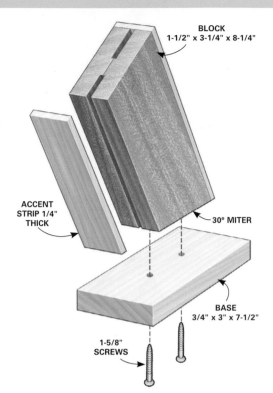

BLOCK
1-1/2" x 3-1/4" x 8-1/4"

ACCENT
STRIP 1/4"
THICK

30° MITER

BASE
3/4" x 3" x 7-1/2"

1-5/8"
SCREWS

Walnut knife rack

YOU probably use one or two knives more than all of your other cutlery combined. So it makes sense to keep your favorite knives handy in a small rack that doesn't take up much counter space.

To build this knife rack, glue two 9-in.-long 1x4s together. Run this glued-up block across a table saw twice to even up the edges. Then measure the blade widths of your knives and set the table saw's blade height 1/8 in. higher than the knife blade widths. Cut slots down the middle of the block (Photo 1). Next, glue 1/4-in.-thick strips to both edges of the block, covering the slots. You can cut the strips from larger stock or buy 1/4-in.-thick material.

Cut one end of the block at 30 degrees (Photo 2). Mount the block on the base with a fast-setting glue such as super glue (Photo 3). Use a gel rather than the liquid. Carefully position the screws so they don't enter the knife slots.

Cost: $15–$25, if made from walnut and maple as shown. Less for other common wood species.

Materials: 2 ft. of walnut 1x4, 2 ft. of maple 1x4, wood glue, fast-setting glue, 1-5/8-in. screws, one can of spray lacquer.

WHAT IT TAKES   **Time:** 1 hour   **Skill level:** Beginner

KNIFE SLOT

FEATHERBOARD

1 Cut knife slots into the block. You have to remove your blade guard, so work carefully. A featherboard clamped to the table saw helps to keep the block tight against the fence.

FENCE

2 Cut the block to length. If you're cutting on a table saw, screw a fence to the miter gauge and clamp the block to the fence. **Warning:** Blade guard removed for photo clarity. Use yours!

3 Mark the block's position with masking tape. Apply fast-setting glue and hold the block in place for one minute. Then add screws for extra strength.

Wren house

Attract wrens and other song-birds to your yard with this durable birdhouse made from a plastic fence post. Wrens will nest in almost any-thing, but other birds have specific requirements for the entrance diam-eter and house cavity. If you're try-ing to attract a particular type of bird to your yard, do a little research online before you start building this rather small hangout.

Buy a 4 x 4-in. fence post and cap kit (sold at home centers). One 6-ft. post is enough for six birdhouses. But the post comes with just one cap, so you'll have to buy caps for all but the first birdhouse.

Cut the house cavity to length and drill the ventilation and entrance holes (Photo 1). Then cut the wood bottom and attach it (Photo 2). Fit the bottom loosely to allow for ven-tilation. To clean out the house each year, just remove the screws and release the bottom. Our birdhouse doesn't include a perch. Perches are cute, but they allow predators easier access to eggs and babies.

Attach the eye hook to the top

WHAT IT TAKES   **Time:** 1 hour
Skill level: Beginner

(Photo 3), then glue the top to the body with a few dabs of polyure-thane glue. If you want to paint the birdhouse, use spray paint formu-lated for plastic, but don't paint the inside of the house.

Hang the houses in partially shaded spots with the entrances facing away from prevailing winds and out of jumping range of cats and squirrels.

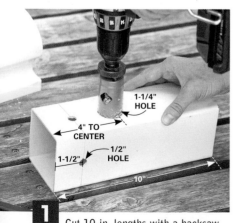

1 Cut 10-in. lengths with a hacksaw or miter saw. Then drill the ventilation and entrance holes. Sand off the sharp edges on the entrance hole with 60-grit sandpaper.

1-1/4" HOLE
4" TO CENTER
1/2" HOLE
1-1/2"
10"

2 Cut a 3/4-in.-thick, 3-1/8-in. square bottom from wood. Predrill and then screw it into place with two No. 8 stainless 3/4-in. pan head screws on opposite sides.

3/4" x 3-1/8" x 3-1/8"
3/4" PAN HEAD SCREWS

3 Drill a 1/4-in. hole for the eye hook and thread on the nut and washer for the top. Stick it through the top and use a needle-nose pliers to hold the bottom nut while you twist the hook tight. Glue on the cap.

3/16" EYE HOOK

Swedish boot scraper

Here's a traditional Swedish farm accessory for gunk-laden soles. The dimensions are not critical, but be sure the edges of the slats are fairly sharp—they're what makes the boot scraper work. Cut slats to length, then cut triangular openings on the side of a pair of 2x2s. A radial arm saw works well for this, but a table saw or band saw will also make the cut. Trim the 2x2s to length, predrill, and use galvanized screws to attach the slats from underneath.

SCREW FROM BELOW

2x2

SLAT

WHAT IT TAKES

Time: 1 hour
Skill level: Beginner

Sliding bookend

To corral shelf-dwelling books or CDs that like to wander, cut 3/4-in.-thick hardwood pieces into 6-in. x 6-in. squares. Use a band saw or jigsaw to cut a slot along one edge (with the grain) that's a smidgen wider than the shelf thickness. Stop the notch 3/4 in. from the other edge. Finish the bookend and slide it on the shelf.

WHAT IT TAKES

Time: 1 hour
Skill level: Beginner

Turned pen holder

On a lathe, turn a 3-in.-square x 6-in.-long hardwood blank into a cylinder that's 4-1/2 in. long with a narrowed waist, curved top and flat bottom. Sand smooth. With a compass, draw a circle on the top and mark six hole locations on the circle. Why six? When you leave the compass at the same radius and "step" it around the circle, it marks off six equally spaced points. After marking, use a 3/8-in. brad point bit to drill the six holes at 10 degrees and 2 in. deep. If your drill press has no angle adjustment, glue three shims together and clamp them to the table to make a 10-degree angled ramp. Finish the pen holder with Danish oil, and load with pens.

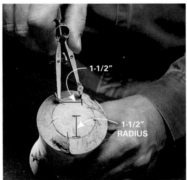

1-1/2"

1-1/2" RADIUS

WHAT IT TAKES

Time: 1 hour
Skill level: Intermediate

Petite shelves

Turn a single 3-ft.-long, 1x12 hardwood board into some small shelves to organize a desk top or counter. Cut off a 21-in.-long board for the shelves, rip it in the middle to make two shelves, and cut 45-degree bevels on the two long front edges with a router or table saw. Bevel the ends of the other board, cut dadoes, which are grooves cut into the wood with a router or a table saw

CUT DADOES BEFORE CUTTING LEGS

with a dado blade, crosswise (cut a dado on scrap and test-fit the shelves first!) and cut it into four narrower boards, two at 1-3/8 in. wide and two at 4 in. Finish, then assemble with brass screws and finish washers.

BEVEL LOWER SHELF EDGES

BRASS SCREWS AND FINISH WASHERS

WHAT IT TAKES

Time: 1 hour
Skill level: Intermediate

5 10 big-impact improvements

Add an outdoor outlet

Most homes have only one or two exterior outlets. That may be OK most of the year, but it's a real hassle when you're doing something like hanging holiday lights. It can be dangerous, too: Overloading cords or outlets poses a fire hazard, while crisscrossing your driveway and sidewalk with cords creates tripping hazards.

In just a few hours, you can solve these problems forever by adding an outlet or two. In this story, we'll show you how to do just that. We've made adding an outlet as easy as possible—simply connect new wire to an existing interior outlet and install your new outlet on the opposite side of the wall. This eliminates the arduous task of fishing wires through finished rooms. To bypass the hassles of cutting a box-size hole in the exterior wall, mount the new outlet right to the siding.

Even if you've never worked with electricity before, you can do this. Our Web site covers all of the basic skills you need to complete this project safely (visit familyhandyman.com). Everything you need is available at home centers for less than $60. Call your local inspections department to apply for a permit before you start.

Choose and mark the outlet location

To keep this project simple, place the new outlet in the same stud cavity as an existing indoor outlet. Start by choosing the interior outlet you want to use. Building codes prohibit tapping into circuits in the kitchen, bathroom, laundry room or into those dedicated to a large appliance, like a refrigerator. You can use living room, bedroom and basement circuits, but don't tap into a circuit that's already overloaded and trips the circuit breaker. To place the outlet somewhere other than opposite the interior outlet, see "Running cable from other power sources," p. 97.

Turn off the circuit breaker controlling the outlet. Use a noncontact voltage tester to be sure the power is off. Then unscrew and pull the receptacle out of the electrical box. Hold the voltage tester over the terminals to

> **WARNING**
> Turn off the power at the main panel, remove the cover plate and outlet, and use a noncontact voltage tester to ensure the power is off.

double-check that the power is off. Next, unscrew the wires from the outlet.

Make sure the junction box is large enough to hold an added set of wires. (An overstuffed box is a fire hazard.) If the box is plastic, shine a flashlight inside and look for a volume listing, such as 21 cu. in. (cubic inches). Then go to familyhandyman.com and type "Adding a receptacle" into the search box to see a chart showing how to determine the minimum box size that's needed. If your box is metal, we recommend that you replace it (see "Replace an electrical box," p. 99). Most metal boxes are too small to hold additional wires.

Use a stud sensor to determine which side of the electrical box the stud is on. Place a 1/4- x 18-in.-long drill bit along the outside of the electrical box on the side away from the stud. Squeeze the bit between the box and the drywall. Don't worry if you make a small hole in the drywall. You can hide it later with the outlet cover plate. Drill through the wall and the siding to mark the location for the new outlet (Photo 1). We tilted the drill bit downward to lower the outlet location (if it's near the ground, you can hide it behind shrubs), but you can place it anywhere on the wall.

Find the marker hole outside and place the exterior junction box over it on the siding. If that's not where you want it, move it straight up or down (within the same stud cavity) and mark the position of the box hole on the siding. Then drill a 1-in. hole over the smaller hole or the mark on the siding to make room for the cable.

If drilling through stucco,

Running cable from other power sources

If you don't want your exterior outlet location limited to where you have interior outlets, you'll have to tap into another electrical circuit. If you have an unfinished basement, you can tap into a junction box in the basement and run the cable out through the rim joist. This is even easier than tapping into a main floor outlet. Plus, it allows you to put your new outlet anywhere, not just opposite an interior outlet. Simply drill a hole through the rim joist and siding, then run a cable from a basement light fixture to the outlet location (Figure A).

A second option is to run wires inside 1/2-in. metal conduit from an existing exterior outlet to the new location (Figure B). The conduit can wrap around corners with a service ell, but don't run it in front of doors. Plant flowers or shrubs in front to cover it.

Figure A
Run a cable from the basement

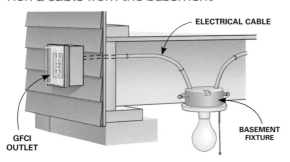

Figure B
Run wires inside conduit

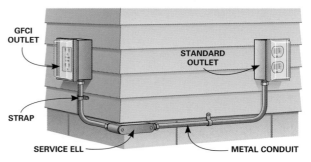

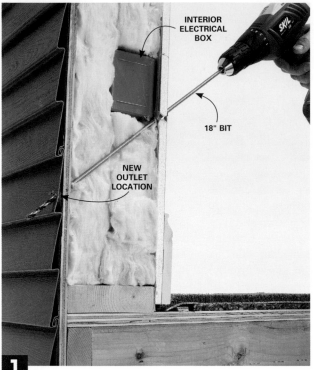

1 Drill a 1/4-in. hole alongside an existing electrical box to mark the location of the new outlet. Go outside and drill a 3/4-in. hole in the siding over or near the smaller hole.

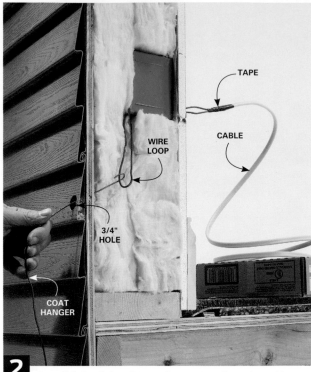

2 Cut off 2 ft. of sheathing and two wires from the cable. Tape the remaining wire to the sheathing, then feed the loop through a knockout in the interior box. Fish for the cable from the exterior hole using a hook made from wire. Pull the cable through the hole.

TIP:

Flat weather-resistant cover on an outdoor receptacle?

Flat covers provide protection only when a receptacle isn't in use, but it's not uncommon for extension cords to be plugged in for extended periods of time; for holiday lights, for example. In-use or "bubble covers" provide protection at all times. The NEC defines a "wet location" as an area that is subject to saturation with water or other liquids, and unprotected locations exposed to the weather. The NEC has another definition for "damp locations" that is more subjective, but if you think the receptacle is going to get wet, use an in-use cover. And don't forget the weather-resistant receptacle. The NEC requires that all 15- and 20-amp receptacles be rated as weather-resistant and tamper-resistant when installed in both wet and damp locations.

Often it's assumed that an exterior outlet that's sheltered by a roof overhang can be covered with one of the older, flap-style outlet covers. But that decision is up to the inspector, so it's better to play it safe and install a bubble cover.

you'll probably wreck the bit, but you'll get through the siding. For brick, use a masonry drill bit with a hammer drill. Then drill a series of small-diameter holes around the marker hole and knock out the center with a hammer and chisel.

Run cable between the outlets

The new wire must be the same gauge (thickness) as the wire already in the box, which is most likely 14 gauge but could be 12. To check, use the labeled notches on wire-stripper pliers.

Run cable from the interior box to the hole in the exterior. Start by removing a knockout in the box by hitting it with a screwdriver. Then strip about 2 ft. of sheathing off the end of the cable and cut off two of the three wires. Tape the end of the remaining wire to the end of the sheathing, forming a loop. Feed the loop through the knockout into the wall cavity.

Bend the end of a wire coat hanger to form a hook. Insert it through the hole in the exterior, grab the wire loop in the wall and pull it back through the hole (Photo 2). Pull through at least 12 in. of cable to give yourself plenty to work with.

Wire the interior outlet

At the interior box, cut the cable so there's 12 in. sticking out, then remove the sheathing to expose the wires. Cut 6-in. pieces of wires from the coil and strip 3/4 in. of insulation off the ends. Screw these short pieces to the

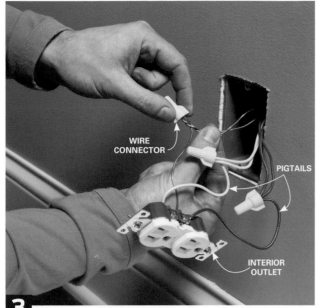

3 Strip 12 in. of sheathing from the cable in the interior box. Strip 3/4 in. of insulation off the ends of the wires. Fasten the pigtail wires to the outlet, then join the wires with wire connectors.

WIRE CONNECTOR
PIGTAILS
INTERIOR OUTLET

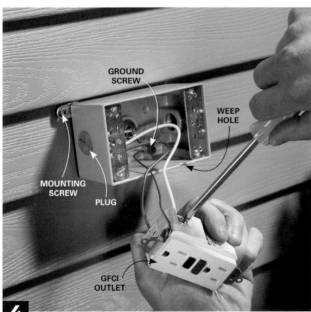

4 Attach a clamp to the box, feed the cable through it into the box, then caulk around the clamp. Mount the exterior outlet box to the house. Wire the outlet and set it in the box.

GROUND SCREW
WEEP HOLE
MOUNTING SCREW
PLUG
GFCI OUTLET

outlet: The bare copper goes to the ground screw (green), the white to either of the silver terminals, and the black to either of the brass screws on the other side. Hook the wires clockwise over the screws so they stay in place as you tighten the screws.

To wire the interior outlet, connect all of the hot wires (black and any other color except green or white), all the neutral wires (white), and all of the ground wires (green or bare copper as shown in Photo 3).

Gently fold the wires into the box, then reattach the outlet and cover plate. If you damaged the wall around the box, use an oversize cover plate to hide the problem.

Replace an electrical box

If your existing electrical box isn't large enough to hold more wires, you'll have to replace it. Remove the old box before cutting a large opening for the new one. This allows you to see if anything is behind the wall before you make the cut.

To swap out boxes, cut the nails that hold the box in place (Photo 1). Then remove the box. Replace it with a plastic "remodeling" box (sold at home centers). These boxes have wings that flip up and attach to the back side of the drywall or plaster. Hold the box over the wall opening and trace around it. Then enlarge the opening with a drywall saw. Don't overcut; you want a snug fit.

Feed the new cable from the outlet being added into the box before installing it (Photo 2). Wrap the cable with electrical tape where the sheathing meets the exposed wires so the sheathing will slide into the box easier.

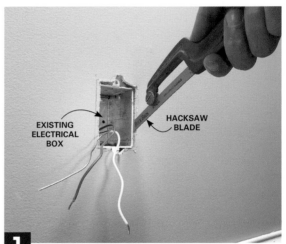

EXISTING ELECTRICAL BOX
HACKSAW BLADE

1 Cut the nails that fasten the box to the stud with a hacksaw blade. Pull out the box and loosen the clamps that hold the wire.

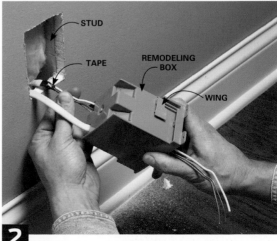

STUD
TAPE
REMODELING BOX
WING

2 Enlarge the wall opening for a remodeling box. Feed in the new and old cables, then mount the box. Caulk any gaps between the box and the wall.

Mount and wire the new outlet

We used a weatherproof receptacle kit (sold at any home center or hardware store) for our exterior outlet. It came with a standard three-prong outlet, but since outside outlets must be GFCI protected, we replaced the kit outlet with a GFCI outlet.

Attach the two mounting lugs to the back of the metal electrical box, putting them in opposite corners. Fasten a clamp to the hole in the back of the box, then feed the cable through the clamp. Apply a heavy bead of silicone caulk around the clamp and place the box on the wall, inserting the clamp into the hole in the siding. The caulk makes the hole watertight. We placed our box horizontally on the lap siding so it could lie flat.

If you have lap siding (wood, hardboard, fiber cement) or plywood sheathing, mount the junction box to the house, using exterior-grade fasteners. Simply drive galvanized deck screws through the mounting lugs. For brick or stucco siding, mount the box with masonry anchors. For vinyl siding over composition board, use hollow wall anchors.

Fasten plugs into the openings on both ends of the box. Use a file to scrape a small notch or "weep hole" in the bottom edge of the box. This allows any water that gets into the box to drain.

Next, strip insulation off the wire ends. Attach the ground wire to the green screw in the box and to the green screw on the GFCI outlet. Make sure to identify the line, hot and white terminals (they'll be labeled "line," "hot" and "white." Attach the black wire to the brass screw or adjacent push-in hole (labeled "line") and the white wire to the silver screw or push-in (Photo 4). Clip

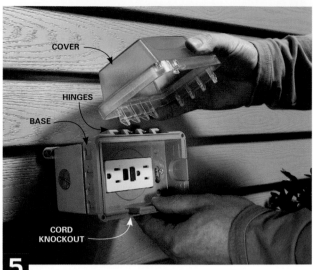

COVER

HINGES

BASE

CORD KNOCKOUT

5 Screw the base to the box. Attach the plastic cover to the base, sliding it over the hinges until it snaps.

the ears off the outlet, fold the wires into the box and set the outlet in place.

You'll need to remove the middle of the plastic base so it'll fit over the GFCI outlet (don't worry, it's designed to come out by twisting it with pliers). Set the base on the box, over the outlet. Make sure the hinges are at the top so the plastic cover will close over the outlet. Fasten the base to the box with the screws that came with the kit.

Attach the cover to the base (Photo 5). Push the hinge receptacles sideways over the hinges until they snap in place. Remove the cord knockouts in the base where the electrical cords will run. Turn the power on and plug in your miles of holiday lights!

Install a programmable thermostat

WHAT IT TAKES

Time: 1 hour
Skill level: Intermediate

You can reduce your home's heating and cooling costs by about 15 percent with a programmable thermostat. It automatically keeps the temperature at a comfortable level when you're home, but switches to an energy-saving level when you're away or asleep. Programmable thermostats are available from home centers and hardware stores for $25 to $100. The higher-priced models provide more programming options.

Programmable thermostats will work with most gas or oil furnaces and central air conditioners. However, heat pumps, electric baseboards and a few other systems require special features. Read the package to make sure the programmable thermostat you buy is compatible with your heating and cooling system. If you're unsure, call your local utility or a heating and cooling contractor.

Remove the old thermostat as shown in Photo 1. If your old thermostat contains mercury, you'll see a small glass tube with a shiny silver ball inside. Mercury is toxic. Take this type of thermostat to a hazardous waste disposal site.

There will be anywhere from two to five wires hooked up to the old thermostat. Label the thermostat wiring with marking tabs using the letters on the old screw terminals as reference. If your new thermostat doesn't come with marking tabs, use masking tape.

Clip a clothespin to the cable so it doesn't slide down inside the wall cavity, and mount the new wall plate (Photo 2). If the thermostat has back-up batteries, insert them before wiring the new thermostat (Photo 3).

The thermostat may need to be configured to your heating system. It may come preprogrammed, but to maximize savings, set it up according to your schedule. Consult the instructions that come with the thermostat for system adjustments and programming. You won't save energy if the thermostat isn't programmed correctly.

Programmable thermostat options

When shopping for a programmable thermostat, select one with the options that are right for you. Some contain a time-to-change-the-filter light or low-battery indicator. Others have keypad lock features to prevent tampering, or contain mechanisms that automatically reset your temperature settings when moving between heating and cooling seasons.

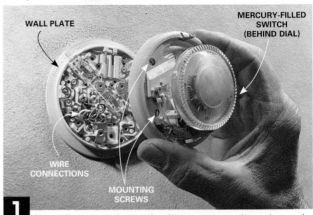

WALL PLATE

MERCURY-FILLED SWITCH (BEHIND DIAL)

WIRE CONNECTIONS

MOUNTING SCREWS

1 Turn off power to heating/cooling systems at the main panel. Mark wires with a tab (or tape) and letter that represents the terminal; unscrew them. Remove and discard the old thermostat.

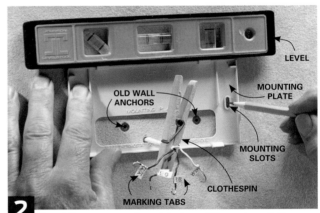

LEVEL

MOUNTING PLATE

OLD WALL ANCHORS

MOUNTING SLOTS

CLOTHESPIN

MARKING TABS

2 Level the new mounting plate in position and mark the mounting screw holes. Drill 3/16-in. holes, insert drywall anchors and screw the plate to the wall.

WIRING

TERMINAL SCREWS

3 Screw wiring to terminals on new thermostat using labels as reference (strip wires back if needed). Hook wires up to same terminals on new thermostat. Snap thermostat to mounting plate.

WHAT IT TAKES

Time: 4 hours
Skill level: Intermediate

Pull the wrinkles out of your carpet

Wall-to-wall carpets sometimes develop loose, wrinkled areas, usually due to installation problems. If you ignore the wrinkles, they'll wear and become permanent eyesores—even if you stretch them later. You don't have to hire a carpet layer—fix it yourself with rental tools and our instructions. Rent a power stretcher and knee kicker for about $40–$50 (for four hours) at an equipment rental store. Then buy a carpet knife (not a utility knife) at any home center.

You'll be stretching from the center of the carpet and pulling it at an angle into a corner. So move any furniture that'll be in the path of the stretch. Loosen the carpet in the corner (Photo 1). Next, set up the power stretcher at an angle across the room. Set the tooth depth on the power stretcher based on the carpet pile depth

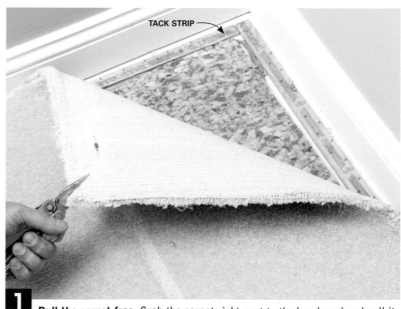

TACK STRIP

1 **Pull the carpet free.** Grab the carpet right next to the baseboard and pull it straight up. Then loosen the rest of the carpet along the wall.

(Photo 2).

Operate the power stretcher with the lever and capture the excess carpet in the tack strip as you stretch. Use the knee kicker on both sides of the locked power stretcher to help lock the carpet into the tacks. Once the wrinkles are out and the carpet is secure in the tack strip, cut off the excess (Photo 4).

3 **Sink and stretch.** Set the teeth into the carpet near the wall and push down on the stretcher handle. Then lock the stretched carpet into place by jamming it behind the tack strip with a putty or linoleum knife.

2 **Dial in the correct tooth depth.** Adjust the tooth depth by loosening or tightening the screws on the spacer bar. Set the bar so the teeth grab just the carpet pile, not the jute backing or pad (the pad is stapled to the floor and shouldn't be stretched).

4 **Trim off excess carpet.** Fold the excess carpet so the backing is facing up. Then cut it off with the carpet knife.

How does carpet get wrinkled?

Carpet has to acclimate to interior conditions before it's installed. That's especially important if the carpet has been in a cold truck or exposed to high humidity. If it's installed while it's still cold or humid, you're going to have wrinkling problems later on.

Improper stretching during installation is another cause. Some installers lay the pad and carpet and secure it with just the knee kicker. Since the carpet was never really stretched, it's going to wrinkle after it's seen some traffic. If the carpet wasn't stretched during installation, it's going to wrinkle later.

Make sure the installers allow enough time for the carpet to acclimate and insist that they actually stretch it with a power stretcher during installation.

Hang a flat-panel TV

Choose the right mount, install it yourself, and save $200

WHAT IT TAKES

Time: 1 hour
Skill level: Beginner

Mounting a flat-panel TV on the wall is one of those jobs where a little know-how can save you a lot of money. Professional installation costs anywhere from $150 to $350—plus the cost of the mount itself. But if you can handle some precise measuring and drive a few screws, you can do a first-class job yourself in about an hour. We'll show you how. Plus, we'll sift through the confusing variety of mounts and help you choose the version that's best for your situation.

Dozens of models, three styles

Don't get overwhelmed by all the wall-mount makes and models. They're all just variations of three basic styles. The three styles differ mainly in how much they allow you to adjust the position of the screen. Adjustments can eliminate glare and increase viewing comfort in other ways too. But adjustability is most important for picture quality. Like a computer screen, the picture on a TV screen is clearest when viewed straight on. So a mount that offers more adjustability gives you a clearer picture in more situations and may even increase your options for where you can place the TV.

Most flat TVs are designed for wall mounting, but make absolutely sure yours is before you shop for a mount. Look for "VESA" (Video Electronics Standards Association) on the manual or the TV itself, followed by a number such as "VESA 75." Any mount with the same VESA number will work with your TV. Also consider wiring before you choose a mount. If you plan to run wiring inside your walls, the mount design may determine how and where you can install an outlet and cable connections.

Three types of mounts

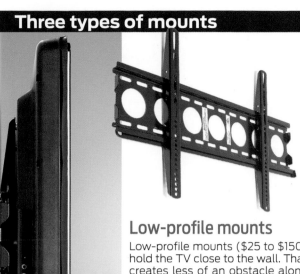

Low-profile mounts

Low-profile mounts ($25 to $150) hold the TV close to the wall. That creates less of an obstacle along traffic paths and reduces the risk of TV damage or bruises. The downside of these mounts is that they don't allow tilting or other adjustments. So if you plan to hang your TV far above eye level, a low-profile mount isn't the best choice. The pricier mounts hold the TV just 1/2 in. from the wall—the less expensive models about 1-1/2 in.

Tilting mounts

Tilting mounts ($50 to $200) let you mount the TV above eye level or tweak the angle to suit the situation—something you may want to do if you're watching TV from the floor one day and the sofa the next. The higher-priced models are easier to adjust and can be set at any angle. Lower-priced models offer a few preset angles and are a bit harder to adjust. That's no problem if you rarely change the angle, but a nuisance if you make frequent adjustments.

Full-motion mounts

Full-motion mounts ($100 to $500) allow you to tilt, swivel, pan and extend the TV. That means you can pull the TV away from the wall and turn it to the left or right, to face the viewer. Full-motion mounts can mount on the wall or in a recessed box as shown. The mount's arm folds into the box, bringing the TV as close to the wall as a low-profile mount would. The box also provides a neat exit point for in-wall wiring.

1 It takes three people to position a TV. When you've found the right spot, mark one corner with masking tape. Set the TV aside and add tape to mark the bottom edge and the other corner.

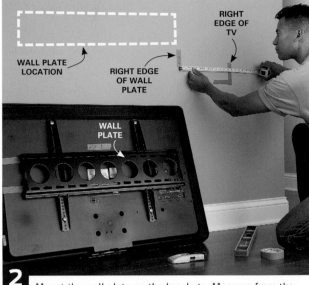

2 Mount the wall plate on the brackets. Measure from the right edge of the TV to the bracket. Transfer the measurement to the wall. Then find the nearest stud and drill.

Get the height right

The most common mistake people make when picking a spot for a TV is placing it too high. Looking up at the screen can give you a sore neck and a murky picture (especially if the TV mount doesn't tilt). Some experts recommend centering the screen at eye level (when you're seated). Others say a bit lower is better, so eye level is centered on the top two-thirds of the TV (that's where most of the on-screen action is).

But there is no "correct" height. A lot depends on the size of the TV and the room. A big TV in a big room can be mounted higher on the wall because the upward viewing angle is decreased when you sit farther from the TV. So the best way to choose the mounting height is with a test drive. This is a three-person job—two to hold the TV and a third to judge the height. Simply get in viewing position and look at the screen in different positions on the wall.

Once you've found the right spot, mark the TV's location on the wall with masking tape (Photo 1). Then set the TV aside and add more tape to mark the bottom edge of the TV on the wall. The tape has to be perfectly level, so use a level to position it. Also locate the centers of the wall studs using an electronic stud finder (the centers of studs provide maximum holding power). If you have concrete, brick or block walls, you can drive screws anywhere. Check the instructions for anchor recommendations.

Position it perfectly

Most wall plates let you slide the TV left or right a few inches, so the plate doesn't have to be perfectly centered where the TV will hang. But positioning the plate at the right height can be tricky. Lots of people end up installing it two or even three times before they get it right. Here's how to avoid wasted time and a wall full of screw holes:

First, screw the brackets to the TV following the instructions. The screw holes in the back of the TV may be hidden by plastic plugs. Just pry them off. Then hang the wall plate on the brackets so the complete mount is attached to the TV. Prop the TV against the wall and measure the distance from the bottom of the TV to the center of each row of mounting holes on the back plate. On the wall, measure the same distances up from the tape and make marks at the stud locations. Check the marks with a level to make sure they're perfectly level (horizontally). Then follow Photo 2.

Drill holes at the marks. The holes should be about 1/8 in. smaller than the lag screws. If the manufacturer didn't include lag screws, check the instructions and pick up the recommended size at a hardware store or home center. Then just screw the plate to the wall using a ratchet wrench and socket.

Mounts are available at electronics stores, home centers, discount stores and online (search for "TV mount").

---

familyhandyman.com
- To run electric lines inside walls, search for "fish wire."
- For tips on hiding speaker cable and other low-voltage lines, search for "hide wire."
- To run electric lines on walls or ceilings, search for "surface wiring."
- To install a whole-house sound system, search for "audio."

Upgrade your car audio

Your factory CD player may work fine. But why put up with a pile of CDs when you can install a brand new MP3 player and listen to all your tunes from a single CD or thumb drive? You can buy a basic MP3 player for about $80 or a full-featured unit for about $200. Save about $40 by installing it yourself. It only takes an hour and it's easy. Just make sure you cough up the $5 or so for car radio removal instructions (search for the term online). Then gather up your tools (screwdrivers, sockets, wire crimpers) and you're ready to rock 'n' roll.

Start the installation by pre-assembling the adapter faceplate (Photo 1). Then attach the stabilizing bracket supplied with the player (if equipped). Next, place the new assembly on your workbench and splice the wiring harness adapter onto the player (Photo 2). Hold the newly assembled unit near the dash and connect the antenna cable and the wiring harness. Then power up the unit and test the speakers. Switch from left to right and front to back to double-check the wiring connections. Test all the player functions (radio, CD player, iPod connection and USB ports). Once you're sure everything works properly, install it in the dash and refasten the trim panels (Photo 3). Then crank up the tunes and rock on.

1 **Build the faceplate.** Assemble the adapter kit. Then insert the MP3 player and secure the entire assembly with the supplied screws.

NEW "POCKET"
OLD RADIO BRACKET

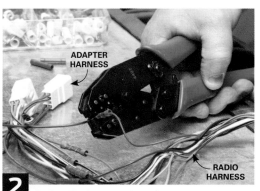

2 **Splice the harness.** Locate the speaker and power wires from the new player and match them to the corresponding wires on the adapter harness. Then crimp (or solder) them together.

ADAPTER HARNESS
RADIO HARNESS

3 **Secure the new unit.** Bolt the new unit into place and attach the stabilizing bracket. Then line up the plastic snaps on any trim panels you removed and tap them back into place.

MP3 shopping tip

You can shop for an MP3 player at any car audio or big-box electronics store. But you'll find a much larger brand and model selection online. Find a model that fits your vehicle and your wallet. Then read the reviews for your selection at online sites. Once you decide on a brand and model, order an installation kit and wiring harness adapter for your particular vehicle (some online sources include the kit for free). Buy red "butt-splice" connectors to connect the harness.

Sealcoat the driveway

You can keep your asphalt in tip-top shape by following the three steps shown here. Asphalt maintenance doesn't require special skills, and you'll only need a few inexpensive tools. You can get everything you need at home centers and hardware stores. However, as with exterior painting, high-quality results hinge on some sweat and careful prep work. Expect to spend about six to eight hours completing the job. To fill cracks and sealcoat an average driveway (750 sq. ft.), you'll spend $100 to $150 on materials. That's about half what a pro would charge.

Fill cracks every year

Maintaining the asphalt skin is the best thing you can do to preserve your

Add a coat of curb appeal

Most driveways are big and conspicuous. And a long stretch of gray, cracking asphalt can give a home a scruffy look, no matter how handsome the rest of the property is. So a fresh coat of shiny black sealer isn't just protection against expensive driveway damage—it's a face-lift for your home and yard.

1 Clean out cracks, digging deep enough to completely remove roots. Clean the edges of the asphalt with a hand broom and blasts of air or water.

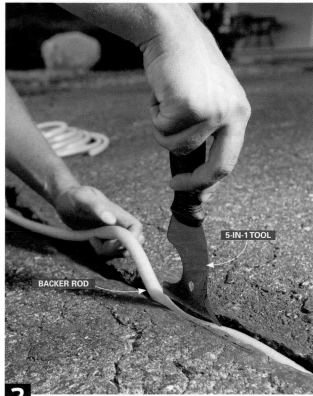

BACKER ROD

5-IN-1 TOOL

2 Stuff backer rod into wide or deep cracks, leaving about 1/2-in. depth to fill with crack filler. The foam rod conserves filler and makes the repair more flexible.

driveway. The asphalt layer serves primarily as a protective skin over the gravel base. The weight of your car is supported by the base, not the asphalt. If too much water gets through, the base erodes, causing additional cracking, potholes and total asphalt breakup.

The best way to keep the asphalt skin intact is to fill cracks, ideally every spring. Buy the high-quality pouring-type filler. Read the labels. Experts recommend the ones containing rubber compounds. They typically handle cracks from 1/8 in. to 1/2 in. wide. For smaller cracks, small tubes of filler in a caulking gun are easier to use. For larger cracks, 1/2 to 3/4 in. wide, buy an extra-thick filler that you spread with a trowel, or tamp in asphalt patching material.

Fillers adhere to the sides of cracks, so your first task is to clean out the dirt and old, loose filler 1/2 in. to 1 in. deep. This is time-consuming. Use a screwdriver or a 5-in-1 tool (shown in Photo 2) for the packed areas. Go deeper if weeds have taken hold. If you don't get all their roots, they'll grow right up through the new filler. Tip: A week before you begin this project, apply a nonselective herbicide to kill roots. Clean the crack edges (Photo 1). You can use a pressure washer or a garden hose, but then let the driveway dry for at least a day before filling.

Fillers need at least 24 hours to dry, so don't fill cracks when rain is in the forecast. The filling technique varies with the product, so check the directions. With most products, you can simply pour the filler into cracks up to 1/4 in. wide. For wider cracks, stuff in backer rod first

(Photo 2). Backer rod is available in several thicknesses at home centers and costs about 10¢ per foot.

Neatness counts when you're filling cracks (Photo 3). The jet-black filler contrasts with the gray asphalt and can look bad if you overfill or smear it.

Cracks that form a spider-web pattern in a small area usually indicate that the base has softened. Water will settle in this spot and make the problem worse. Fillers will help for a while, but sooner or later you'll have to cut out and patch the cracked area. Cut the asphalt using a diamond blade in your circular saw (Photo 4). Then repack the gravel base by pounding it with a 6-ft. 4x4 or a hand tamper. Fill the cutout and pack with a 4x4 or hand tamper (Photo 5).

You can buy asphalt patching material at home centers and hardware stores, but it isn't nearly as durable as regular hot asphalt. For better performance, sealcoat the patch after about six months. And for areas larger than a few square feet, hire a pro.

Clean up edges every two years

Asphalt edges are especially prone to cracking because the base erodes at edges more easily. Grass invades the cracks and increases erosion. So every other year, grab a shovel or lawn edger and cut back the grass (Photo 6). Then clean out and fill the cracks.

Sealcoat every four to five years

The purpose of a sealcoat is to protect the asphalt against

3 Pour in filler until it's even with the driveway surface. Smooth out overfilled areas with a putty knife. Check for voids in the filler the next day and refill them.

4 Saw around heavily cracked areas using a circular saw and diamond blade. Chisel out all the loose asphalt down to the gravel base.

sun and water and to fill small cracks. It also dresses up the asphalt by covering fillers and patches. You don't need to do it every year. In fact, sealcoat will peel if there are too many layers, and you'll permanently ruin the appearance of the driveway.

Home centers carry several sealers. Buy the best one (the most expensive!), especially if you're sealing your driveway for the first time. A better sealer means better long-term adhesion. Adhesion is vital, because you'll apply more coats in future years, and each fresh coat is only as good as the coat beneath it.

To ensure good sealer adhesion, the driveway must be clean and dry. Fill cracks and edge the driveway at least a week in advance. Scrub with a stiff broom. Then sweep or blow debris off with a leaf blower. You can use a garden hose or a pressure washer, but you'll have to wait for it to dry.

Sealer won't stick to oily spots left by a drippy car. First scrape off the oily gunk with a putty knife. Then apply a detergent (such as dishwashing liquid) or buy the sealer manufacturer's cleaner and scrub. After you rinse, examine the spot. If you see an oil film on the rinse water or if water beads up on the spot, scrub again. You can wash the entire driveway surface at this time, since you'll have to wait one or two days for the asphalt to dry anyway. When it's dry, apply primer (Photo 7) to the spots.

5 Fill the cutout with new asphalt. Be sure to repack the gravel base first. Then add asphalt in 1-in. layers, packing each layer with a hand tamper.

HAND TAMPER

Before you apply sealer, check the weather forecast and the sealer's label to make sure you'll get good drying conditions. Sealcoats are water-based, and a rainfall before they dry will ruin them. Drying times will slow in cooler and more humid conditions.

Coat the edges first using a stiff brush such as a masonry brush (Photo 8). Then coat the entire driveway using a sealcoating broom or squeegee (Photo 9). Stir the sealer before application even if the label claims it's a no-mix formula. Sealcoating isn't difficult, but it is messy. Wear old shoes and clothing you can toss. The worst mistake is stepping in drips, then tracking the sealcoat across concrete or inside your home.

TIP:
If you're a rookie, work on a cooler, more humid day to slow drying so you have more time to spread the sealer smoothly.

6 Cut back invading grass along the driveway. Left alone, grass roots will enlarge any cracks and gradually destroy the driveway from the edges inward.

7 Coat oil-stained spots with a primer before sealcoating. Without thorough cleaning and primer, the sealcoat won't stick to oily areas.

8 Apply the sealer around the perimeter of the driveway. Protect walls and the adjacent concrete with wide masking tape.

9 Spread the sealer by working back and forth across the driveway. Pull the broom or squeegee at an angle to plow the excess sealer onto the uncoated area.

Be sure to read the manufacturer's directions and follow the recommended spread rate. Take care not to lay it on too thick. Puddles or thick areas will probably peel. Work the sealer into the surface. Although some sealers require only one coat, it's better to have two thin coats than one thick coat. And you're less likely to leave ridges or brush marks.

Finally, surround the driveway with stakes and string or tape. Keep everyone, including pets, off the finished surface until it dries. Otherwise you might find black, gooey paw or foot prints on your kitchen floor!

familyhandyman.com
- To see how pros install a whole new driveway, go to familyhandyman.com and search for "driveway."
- For concrete repair help, go to familyhandyman.com and search for "concrete repair."
- Driveway sinking in front of the garage? For a do-it-yourself solution go to familyhandyman.com and search for "sinking driveway."

Install a new sink and faucet

Installing a new sink and faucet is easier than ever thanks to the simple-to-cut-and-assemble white plastic (PVC) drain parts (Photo 7) and nearly foolproof flexible water supply tubes (Photo 6). Some plumbing experience would be helpful, but even without it you can replace your sink and faucet in less than a day using a few basic tools that you probably already own. You'll need large slip-joint pliers for the drain fittings (Photo 1), a fine-tooth saw to cut the plastic pipe, a set of open-end wrenches or two adjustable wrenches to loosen and tighten the supply tubes, and hex head nut drivers for the sink clips and the clamp on the dishwasher drain. If you have a plastic laminate countertop and need to enlarge the hole for the new sink, you'll also need a jigsaw.

WHAT IT TAKES

Time: 1 day
Skill level: Intermediate

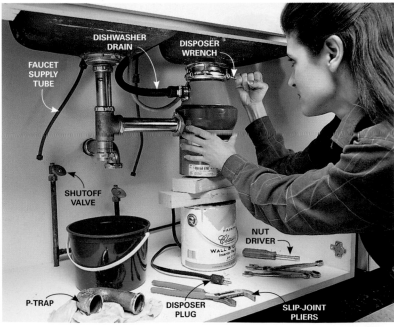

FAUCET SUPPLY TUBE

DISHWASHER DRAIN

DISPOSER WRENCH

SHUTOFF VALVE

NUT DRIVER

P-TRAP

DISPOSER PLUG

SLIP-JOINT PLIERS

1 Remove the trap and other drain parts by loosening the slip-joint nuts with large slip-joint pliers or a pipe wrench. Disconnect the disposer from the sink by sticking a large screwdriver or disposer wrench into the ring near the drain and twisting it counterclockwise. You may have to tap it with a hammer to break it free. Close the water valves and disconnect the tubes leading to the faucet. Hold the shutoff valve steady with one wrench while you loosen the supply tube nut with a second wrench. Remove any clips holding the sink in and lift it out.

The key to simplicity:
Buy a new sink the same size as the old

Measure your old sink. The standard size is 33 x 22 in. and about 7 in. deep. If yours is this size, you'll have no problem finding a new one to fit the same hole. If you want to install a sink that's larger or deeper than your current one, first check the cabinet width below to make sure it'll fit. Then decide how to enlarge the hole. If your countertop is stone, tile, solid surface or metal, you may have to hire a pro to enlarge the hole. If it's wood or plastic laminate, enlarge the hole yourself with a jigsaw.

Tips for removing the old sink

Getting the old sink out is usually harder than putting the new one in. Old plumbing parts are likely to be corroded, and the sink may be glued to the counter with caulk or caked-on gunk. Sinks are mounted in several ways, but

2 Mount the new faucet to the new sink. Follow the instructions provided with your faucet. Protect your countertop with cardboard.

NEW FAUCET

FAUCET INSTRUCTIONS

NEW SINK

Parts and supplies

- Plumber's putty
- Tub-and-tile caulk
- Two basket strainer assemblies (only one if you're installing a disposer)

You'll need the following 1-1/2-in. PVC drain parts:

- One P-trap assembly
- One end or center outlet waste kit
- Two sink tailpieces—only one if you're installing a disposer. If you have a dishwasher and no disposer, get a special "dishwasher" tailpiece that has a tube to connect the dishwasher drain hose.
- One special "disposer" waste arm, if you have a disposer
- Two flexible water supply tubes for kitchen sinks. Match the nuts on the ends to the threads on your faucet and shutoff valves. Also measure to determine the right length.

3 Set your new sink in the countertop to check the fit, then trace around it with a pencil. Enlarge the hole if necessary. Remove the sink and apply a bead of mildew-resistant tub-and-tile caulk just to the inside of the pencil line. Set the sink back in the hole and use a nut driver to tighten the clips that hold the sink down. Tighten the clips just enough to close the gap between sink and countertop. Don't overtighten. Clean up the excess caulk with a damp cloth.

TUB-AND-TILE CAULK

SINK CLIPS

PLUMBER'S PUTTY

DISPOSER DRAIN

BASKET STRAINER CUP

4 Roll plumber's putty into a 1/2-in.-dia. rope and form it around each drain opening. Press the top half of the basket strainer assembly down into the plumber's putty on one side. On the other, press the disposer drain down into the putty.

5 Assemble the undersink half of the basket strainer assembly and tighten the large nut with slip-joint pliers. Hold the basket with your hand to keep it from spinning. Reassemble the disposer drain and tighten the three screws. Clean the excess plumber's putty from around the drain openings and polish the sink with a dry cloth.

6 Connect the water supply valves to the new faucet with flexible braided stainless steel sink connectors. Hand-tighten the connections. Then turn them an additional quarter turn with a wrench.

here are a few general tips for removing yours:

■ Place a bucket under the trap to catch wastewater while you loosen the slip-joint nuts.

■ Remove the disposer (Photo 1).

■ Use a pair of pipe wrenches to separate drain parts that won't yield to large slip-joint pliers. Don't worry about damaging the pipes; you'll be replacing them with new plastic parts anyway.

■ Add shutoff valves if your hot and cold water supply pipes don't have them.

■ Working carefully, slice the caulk around the sink with a utility knife, then slip a stiff putty knife under the sink's lip and gently pry up to loosen it. On some old sinks, you must remove the mounting clips from under the sink before you lift it out.

■ Get help lifting out a cast iron sink.

Save your back

Prop up a scrap of plywood on some 1-qt. paint cans in front of the cabinet or grab a big bag of pet food. This will make working under the sink more comfortable.

Otherwise, the edge of the cabinet would be digging into your back.

Tips for installing the new sink

Follow the steps in Photos 2 – 7 to assemble, install and connect your new sink and faucet. Some sinks, like the stainless steel sink shown here, require clips tightened from below to hold them in place (Photo 3). Most cast iron sinks are held in place by their own weight and a bead of caulk. Follow the mounting instructions provided with your sink.

When you're finished with the installation, turn on the shutoff valves and check for leaks. Then run water in both bowls and check the drains for leaks. Most leaks can be fixed by tightening the connection. If this doesn't work, you'll have to take the leaky joint apart and inspect it for missing or misaligned parts.

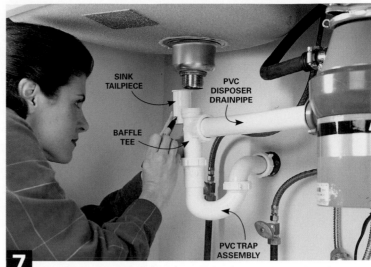

SINK TAILPIECE

PVC DISPOSER DRAINPIPE

BAFFLE TEE

PVC TRAP ASSEMBLY

7 Loosely assemble the new PVC drain fittings. Hold up and mark parts needing to be cut. Then saw them with a fine-tooth wood saw or hacksaw. Slope the horizontal pipes down slightly toward the drain in the wall. Hand-tighten all the fittings and turn the nuts an additional quarter turn with large slip-joint pliers.

Get the job done FASTER

Repairing water damage

Let's face it—it's easy to get water on the floor of your sink base cabinet. We'll never understand why cabinetmakers use particleboard for the base, but they do. And once it starts swelling, your only option is to replace it. But you don't have to cut out the entire bottom. Here's an easier way to install a new sink base bottom.

Remove the drain lines (and garbage disposer, if there is one) to get maneuvering room. Then trace a cutting line about 3 in. in from all four edges. Then cut out the middle section of the swollen sink base with a jigsaw (Photo 1). Next, cut a piece of 1/2-in. plywood to the interior size of the sink base. Cut slots for the water supply tubes. Then seal the edges and face of the plywood with urethane varnish. Then install the new plywood floor and fasten it to the old floor (Photo 2). Caulk around the edges and pipes to prevent water from seeping under the new floor. Then reattach the P-trap and garbage disposer.

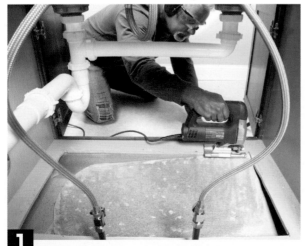

1 **Remove the middle section.** Drill a 3/4-in. hole in each corner of the traced cutout line. Then run your jigsaw along the line. Remove the old, swollen floor.

2 **Drop in the new floor and screw it into place.** Predrill holes around the perimeter using a countersink bit. Then install brass-colored drywall screws.

Restore a garage floor

A fresh new face for ugly concrete in one day!

If your slab is suffering from low self-esteem because of pits, craters or cracks, you can cover up those scars. Concrete "resurfacer" is a cement-based coating that forms a smooth, new surface right over the old concrete. The cost of resurfacer for a two-car garage is typically less than $200. You'll also need to buy or rent some special tools, so expect your total cost to be about $300.

Clearing out your garage so you can work may take weeks! However, cleaning and resurfacing usually goes quickly. Spreading the resurfacer smoothly is the trickiest part of the project, so it helps to have some experience with concrete or drywall finishing. Cool weather, with temps in the 60s, also helps. Warmer weather makes resurfacer harden faster, reducing the time you have to finish the surface.

WHAT IT TAKES

Time: 1 day
Skill level: Intermediate

Gather your materials

Everything you'll need for this project is available at home centers. Aside from basic tools like a hammer and chisel, buckets and a steel trowel, you'll need:

Resurfacer: Home centers sell concrete resurfacer under various brand names. To estimate the amount you need, check the label and then buy two or three extra containers. Better to return some than to run out before the job's done.

Plastic sheeting: Protect walls with a band at least 3 ft. high. We used 6-mil plastic, but lighter stuff will work too.

Concrete cleaner: We used concrete and stucco wash. Various brands are available.

Brush: A stiff version designed for stripping decks and mounted on a handle will keep you off your knees.

Pressure washer: For thorough cleaning, you'll need a model with 3,000 psi and a 15-degree spray tip. Rent one for four hours.

Squeegee: Get a beefy version designed for floors, not a lightweight window-cleaning tool. A quality squeegee will give you better results and is worth the price.

Mixing equipment: A powerful 1/2-in. drill and a mixing attachment are the only way to go. Mixing by hand is too slow.

Protective gear: Rubber boots and gloves protect your skin against the degreaser and resurfacer (which can burn skin). You'll also need eye and hearing protection.

Results to expect

As a first-timer, you might achieve a perfectly smooth, flat finish. Or you might end up with a few rough spots and small ridges. But even if your work is far from flawless, you'll still make a bad floor look much better. And remember this: If you make some major mistakes, you can add a second coat—this time with the benefit of experience.

Resurfacer is tough stuff that will withstand decades of traffic. It will permanently fill craters, but with cracks, long-term success is hard to predict. Tight, stable cracks may reappear. Cracks that have shifted slightly with the seasons or gradually widened over the years probably will reappear. That doesn't mean you shouldn't resurface the floor—even a crack that reappears and gradually grows will look a lot better than one that's left alone.

Prep the slab

The cleaner the concrete, the better the resurfacer will stick. Start with a thorough sweeping. If you have oil spots to clean, scrub them with a deck brush and concrete cleaner. Once you've removed the stains, apply cleaner to the whole slab with the brush. Then fire up the pressure washer (Photo 1). Start in the back of the garage and work your way to the front, forcing the excess water out the overhead doorway.

Important: If you find that the cleaner doesn't soak into the concrete but just beads up into droplets on the surface, you have a sealer over the concrete that you'll need to remove. In that case, apply a stripper first to remove the sealer, then clean.

When the slab is clean, look for any pieces of concrete that the sprayer may

What it takes

Time: One to two days
Cost: Around $300
Skill level: Intermediate
Tools: Hammer, chisel, pressure washer, trowel, drill, mixer, squeegee

1 **Start with a clean floor:** Scrub with a concrete degreaser and a stiff brush, then follow up with a pressure washer. Rinse twice to remove all residue.

2 **Remove the loose stuff:** Chisel away any loose fragments along cracks or craters; there's no need to bust away concrete that's firmly attached.

have loosened. Chip these away (Photo 2) and collect the debris as you go, sweeping it into a dustpan with an old paintbrush. Now's the time to fill these cracks or divots. Mix some resurfacer to a mashed potato–like consistency and push the mix into the cracks. Smooth it with a cement trowel flush with the surrounding surface (Photo 3).

If you have expansion joints cut into the existing slab, push a weather strip into the joint. This will maintain the joint and give you a convenient time to stop and take a break. Apply and smooth no more than 150 sq. ft. of resurfacer at a time for the best results. You can glue a length of weather strip to the slab to define a stopping point if you don't have a control joint and then continue from that edge once you've smoothed the first section.

For a nice-looking finished edge under the overhead door, apply a heavy-duty vinyl weather strip (Photo 4) (sold at home centers). Just be sure to dry the slab along the location with a hair dryer so your adhesive will work properly.

Erase your mistakes

If you end up with ridges, shallow craters or squeegee marks, you don't have to live with them forever. Go to a rental store and rent a concrete grinder. It looks like a floor polisher, but it grinds down the surface, removing about 1/16 in. with each slow pass. It's a dusty job that might take all day, but you'll get a much smoother, flatter surface—perfect if you want to apply a finish like epoxy paint.

3 **Fill cracks and craters:** Mix up a stiff batch of resurfacer, using just enough water for a workable consistency. Scrape off the excess so repairs are flush with the surrounding floor.

GARAGE DOOR WEATHER STRIP

4 **Create a dam:** Glue weather strip to the floor exactly where the garage door rests. This will stop resurfacer from flowing onto the driveway.

Mix and spread the resurfacer

This is the time to recruit a helper. You'll need one person to mix and another to spread resurfacer. Take two minutes to read the directions before mixing. The key to a smooth, lump-free mix is to let the resurfacer "slake," that is, sit in the bucket for a few minutes after the initial mixing. Then mix a bit more (Photo 5). It's also good to have a slat of wood on hand to scrape the sides of the bucket as you mix.

The concrete should be damp when you apply the resurfacer, but not wet to the touch. Pour the mix onto the slab and immediately spread it (Photo 6). Work quickly and carefully, blending each stroke into the previous one until you get a nice, uniform look. Smooth the resurfacer along the side walls by pulling the squeegee toward you. As you reach the edge of the door weather strip, use your steel trowel to gently blend the resurfacer against the weather strip. You can remove the excess with the trowel and drop it into a bucket.

With the slab finished, let the mix set up. In hot, dry weather, it's a good idea to mist the hardened surface; keeping it damp longer will allow the resurfacer to fully harden. After several hours, the finish will support foot traffic. Depending on the weather, wait at least 24 hours before driving on your newly finished slab. After a few days of curing, you can apply a sealer if you'd like to protect the slab from oil and other stains.

5 **Mix like mad:** Recruit a helper to mix the resurfacer while you spread it. The material begins to stiffen quickly, so the faster you get it all mixed and applied, the better your results.

6 **Spread it smooth, then let it set:** Push the squeegee forward to work the resurfacer into the concrete, then drag it back to smooth the coating. Aim for a thickness of 1/8 in. When you've covered the whole floor, let it cure for 24 hours before you drive on it.

Install a new storm door

WHAT IT TAKES

Time: 4 hours
Skill level: Intermediate

You no longer have to put up with a rusty old storm door that bangs shut every time the kids go out. In fact, installing a new one is one of the least expensive ways to dress up an entry.

Replacing an old storm door is easier than you might think. Manufacturers have made installation more DIY friendly by providing standard sizes that'll fit almost any door opening and simpler installation kits. Still, you'll find some sticking points. The following step-by-step directions walk you through some tricks and techniques you won't find in any instruction manual.

If you have a hacksaw, screw gun, a short level and a pair of side cutters and two to three hours, you're on your way to saving the cost of a professional installation.

1 Pick a flat area near the entry door, lay the box flat on the ground, fold it open and check to make sure you have all the parts.

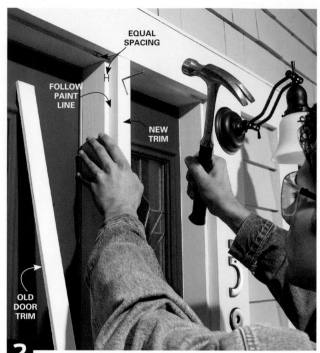

2 Add a trim extension if needed to doors with sidelights. Prime and paint the new trim, position it with a reveal equal to the other trim and then nail it into place.

> **TIP:**
> If your entry door trim needs paint, do it now. It's a pain in the neck painting around a new door, and you'll have a crisper-looking job.

Replacing an old storm door or installing a new one is a perfect Saturday morning project, even if you have limited carpentry skills. Choose a storm door that fits the style of your home. Prices range from $100 to $300.

Selecting the door

To find the size of the storm door you need, simply measure the height and width of the main door. Most front entry doors are 36 in. wide and require a 36-in. storm door.

Here a "full-view" storm door was chosen (opening photo). The one shown has a removable screen and glass panels that you interchange each season. The other common type, a "ventilating" storm door, has glass panels that slide open or closed over the screen, much like a double-hung window.

Nearly every storm door sold is reversible. That is, you can install it with the hinge on either side. The manufacturer's directions tell you how to do it. When you buy it, you don't have to specify which way the door must swing.

You typically mount storm doors to the exterior door trim using "Z-bars." The hinge-side Z-bar may already be screwed to the door as this one was, or you may have to mount it once you determine the door swing direction. On some doors, you'll also have to drill holes for the latch.

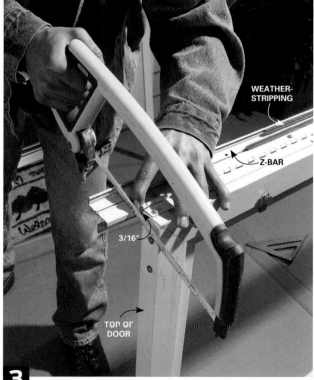

3 Confirm the door swing direction and fasten the hinge-side Z-bar to the correct side (if necessary). Mark a cutting line on the Z-bar 3/16 in. above the top of the door with a square. Slide the weatherstripping aside and cut the Z-bar with a hacksaw.

> **TIP:**
> Use an 18- to 22-tooth-per-inch hacksaw blade for smoother, easier cuts.

4 Measure from the outside lip of the threshold to the top door casing. Transfer the measurement to the bottom of the hinge-side Z-bar and cut it to length, matching the angle on the threshold.

Getting started

Begin the project by folding open the box and removing the glass storm panel. Set it and the screen panel in a safe place out of the wind. Then check for damaged or missing parts by comparing the contents with the parts list in the instruction manual. (This door had been returned, repackaged and sold as new. One of the parts had already been cut to length and the mounting screws were missing.) Use the cardboard as a work surface to prevent scratching the parts while you work on the door. Then determine the door swing. In general, hinge the storm door on the same side as the main door. However, consider these exceptions:

■ **Adjoining walls.** If there's an adjoining wall or rail, it's best to have the door swing against it; otherwise entry can be awkward, especially if you're carrying groceries.

■ **Electrical.** Will the door open against any light fixtures? Will the doorbell or light switch wind up on the latch side where they belong?

■ **Wind.** If there's a strong prevailing wind, it's best to have the door hinge side face the wind direction. That way, sudden gusts can't fling it open and break it.

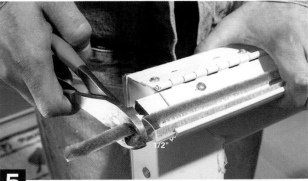

5 Center the weatherstripping in the Z-bar, then snip off the ends, leaving it 1/2 in. extra long at each end.

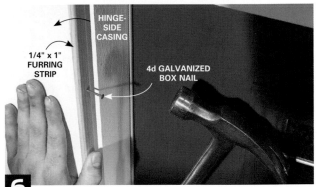

6 Measure the opening width and determine the furring strip thickness (see text). Cut a furring strip to length, then nail it to the inside edge of the hinge-side casing with four evenly spaced 4d galvanized box nails.

7 Lift the door into the opening and pry it against the hinge-side casing with a twist from rubber-handled pliers on the latch side. Screw the hinge Z-bar into the door casing side.

Why a storm door?

A traditional storm door was a real workhorse. It protected the handsome but vulnerable wooden main door from harsh weather and helped to insulate it.

Today's better insulated and protected main doors have little need for a storm door and are often elimi-nated from new homes, showing off fancy front doors. However, the "full-view" storm door (like the one shown here) still showcases the main door and, when screened, allows you to take advantage of those cooling summer breezes too.

8 Swing the door open, slip the top-side Z-bar into place and close the door to hold it. Adjust the gap between the Z-bar and the top of the door until it's even and screw it into the top casing.

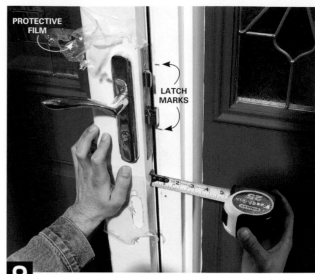

9 Mount the latch mechanism, then mark the position of the top and bottom of the latch on the door casing. If the space between the door and the casing is over 5/8 in., nail two 1/4-in.-thick furring strips to the inside of the casing, one above and one below the marks (see Photo 11).

10 Hold the latch-side Z-bar against the open door and center the holes on the latches. Then push the door and Z-bar against the door frame and mark and cut the bottom at the angle of the threshold. Then mark the top (inset) and cut it.

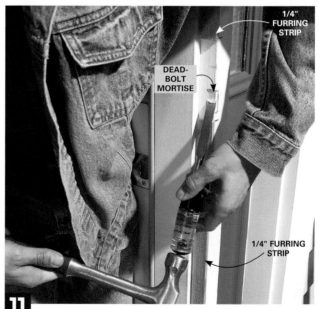

11 Close the door against the casing with the dead-bolt extended and chisel out the wood where the deadbolt hits. Slip the latch-side Z-bar into place, close the door against it and screw it to the casing, keeping a consistent 1/8-in. gap with the door.

Out with the old storm door

Taking off an old aluminum door is usually just a case of unscrewing the mounting screws on the door, closer and safety chain. But sometimes there's caulk around the frame. You can usually cut through the caulk with a utility knife. But worse yet, you could find old caulk between the frame and the door casing. If so, you'll have to pry the frame away with an old chisel and scrape the trim surfaces clean. A heat gun may help soften the caulk.

Wooden storm doors generally have hinges that are mortised (notched into the wood) and screwed to the door casing. Don't worry about the hinge or latch recesses. When you install your new storm door, they'll be hidden behind the new door frame.

Prep the opening

Storm doors hang from the door trim, technically called "exterior casing." If the door has never had a storm door, you may have to extend the trim between the door and a sidelight (Photo 2). This is the most difficult situation you're likely to encounter. You have to rip a new trim piece to match the thickness of the other trim (usually 1-1/8 in. thick).

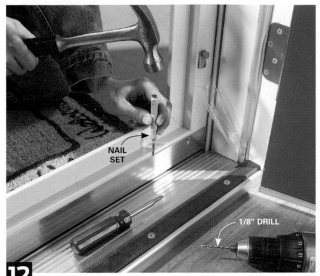

12 Slide the rubber weatherstripping into the door sweep and crimp the ends. Slide the sweep over the door bottom and tap it down to snug it to the threshold. Drill 1/8-in. holes through the adjustment slots and add the screws.

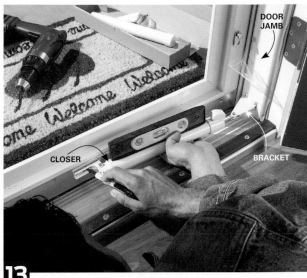

13 Position the closer bracket and screw it to the jamb. Attach the closer, level it and mark the screw positions on the door. Drill 1/8-in. pilot holes and screw the closer to the door. Repeat for the top closer.

Manufacturers make storm doors a bit narrower than standard openings to make sure they'll fit. If your opening is typical, you'll have to "fur out" the sides to center the storm door in the opening. You'll nearly always need to install at least one 1/4-in. furring strip on the hinge side (Photo 6) and possibly even have to add another one to the latch side (Photo 11). To figure this out, measure the exact width of the opening, that is, the distance between the inside edges of the trim. (Measure at the middle, top and bottom.) The manufacturer's instructions will usually list the minimum width required. Subtract that width from your measurement and make the furring strip thickness along the hinge side about half the difference.

It's important to mount the door tightly to the hinge-side trim. Pry against the latch side to make sure it snugs up tight (Photo 7).

Follow the photos with your instructions for the rest of the installation steps. Door latch and Z-bar systems vary. Cutting the latch-side Z-bar is a bit fussy. The idea is to center it on the latch and lock (Photo 10). Observe where it strikes the sill and cut the bottom at an angle that matches the sill. Then cut the top so it fits against the top Z-bar. Don't worry if the latch and lock bolt end up a bit off-center, as long as they work smoothly.

You may need to chisel out the latch or deadbolt pocket as shown (Photo 11). It all depends on the door latch style.

After installing the door sweep and closers, adjust the closer tension. Begin with the window panel rather than the screen in place. The closers should be set with the door at its heaviest. You may want to reset a gentler setting for the screen panel.

Finally, it's a good idea to save the boxes for the window and screen panel for off-season storage. Under a bed is a great safe storage location.

Dealing with warped doors

Storm doors often appear to be warped because they don't rest evenly against the weatherstripping at all corners. However, it's usually the entry door trim that's a bit out of whack. Small gaps may disappear when you install the door closers, especially if your door comes with one for the top and one for the bottom. If that doesn't do the trick, try prying out the Z-bar slightly and slip in a shim (photo below) that should close the gap.

Bigger gaps call for more drastic measures. First loosen all the Z-bar screws and remove the screws at opposite corners of the door. Then slip a shim behind the corner screws, opposite the gap. Tighten the corner screws to see if the gap closes. Try varying sizes of shims until the door closes well. Then slip in progressively smaller shims behind the rest of the screws as you tighten them to taper the gap between the Z-bar and the door casing. Cut off the shims, then caulk the gap and paint it to match.

Replace a toilet
Tips for a trouble-free, leak-free installation

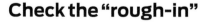

WHAT IT TAKES — **Time:** 4 hours — **Skill level:** Intermediate

Whether you're installing a better-flushing toilet or resetting the old one after repairs or remodeling, these tips will help you do it faster and with fewer problems. The job can take less than an hour, but set aside a whole morning in case you run into trouble. Everything you'll need is available at home centers and hardware stores.

Brass bolts are best

Some metal toilet bolts have a yellowish zinc coating that makes them look like brass. So check the label and make sure you're getting brass bolts and nuts. They won't rust away and they're easier to cut off later. If you need to re-anchor the toilet flange (see p. 128), buy stainless steel screws. They won't corrode like steel or break off like brass while you're driving them.

Check the "rough-in"

If you're buying a new toilet, you need to know the "rough-in" measurement of the old one. For the vast majority of toilets, the waste pipe is centered about 12 in. from the wall. But with a few models, that measurement is 10 in. or 14 in. To check the rough-in, just measure from the wall to the toilet's hold-down bolts. If that measurement (plus the thickness of the baseboard) isn't approximately 12 in., toilet shopping will be a bit harder. Most home centers carry only one or two 10-in. models and no 14-in. models. If you have to special-order a toilet, be prepared to spend much more.

If there's a door near the toilet, also measure how far the bowl protrudes from the wall. If you replace a standard bowl with an "elongated" model, the door may not close.

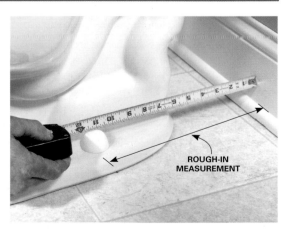

ROUGH-IN MEASUREMENT

Cut hold-down bolts

Don't be surprised if the old nuts that hold the toilet in place won't budge. Years of corrosion can weld them to their bolts. In that case, a hacksaw blade is the solution. You can buy a "close quarters" blade holder at home centers and hardware stores, or just wrap a bare blade with a rag or duct tape. Most toilet bolts and nuts are brass, so they're easy to cut. If the bolt spins, grab it with locking pliers as you cut.

Sit a bit to squish the wax

When you set the toilet in place, you have to squish the wax ring until the toilet settles to the floor. DON'T force the toilet down by tightening the nuts on the toilet bolts—that might crack the porcelain base. Instead, sit on the toilet backward with your weight centered over the wax ring. Then wiggle your bottom until the toilet reaches the floor. But don't go wild. You want to drive the toilet straight down with minimal twisting or shifting of it from side to side. When the toilet reaches the floor, snug down the toilet bolt nuts.

Eliminate rocking with shims

A toilet that rocks on an uneven floor will eventually break the wax ring seal and leak. So check for wobbles after you've set the toilet in place and loosely tightened the nuts. For slight wobbles, slip coins or stainless steel washers into the gaps under the toilet. Don't use regular steel washers, which might rust and stain the floor. For larger gaps, use shims. There are plastic shims made especially for toilets, but plastic construction shims like the ones shown here work just as well. When you've eliminated the wobble, tighten the nuts, cut off the shims and caulk around the toilet base. A toilet set on thick vinyl flooring can loosen as the vinyl compresses. In that case, just retighten the nuts a few days after installation.

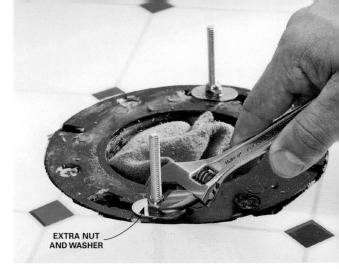

EXTRA NUT AND WASHER

Lock down the bolts

Setting a toilet onto the new bolts can be the most frustrating part of the whole installation. The bolts slip and tip as you're straining to align them with the holes in the toilet. And each time you miss, you risk crushing or shifting the wax ring. The plastic slip-on washers sometimes included with bolts help, but they still allow the bolts to move. The best approach is to buy a second set of nuts and washers so you can lock the bolts in place before you set the toilet. To make sure they're in the correct position, set the toilet and check its height and position. Then lift it off and add the wax ring. To make the bolts easier to find, mark their locations with masking tape.

Don't overtighten the water connections

Do yourself a favor and buy a flexible water supply line. They're a lot easier to install than stiff metal or plastic tubing. Be sure to get one that's covered with stainless steel mesh. For a good seal, hold the hose so it aims straight into the shutoff or fill valve while you're screwing on the connectors. Make them hand-tight, then add another quarter turn with pliers. Connections that are too tight can actually cause leaks or spin the fill valve inside the tank. Check for leaks and tighten them a bit more if needed.

Cut the bolts last

To make positioning a toilet easier, new toilet bolts are extra long. That means you have to cut off the protruding ends later with a hacksaw. But first connect the water line, flush the toilet a couple of times and check for leaks. Leaving the bolts uncut until you've done these final checks lets you easily remove and reset the toilet if you find any problems.

After cutting, double-check the bolts for tightness. Cutting often loosens the nuts a bit.

Flange fixes

A rock-solid toilet flange is the key to a leak-free toilet. The flange is the only thing anchoring the toilet to the floor. If the flange is loose or damaged, the toilet will rock. And a rocking toilet will distort the wax ring and cause leaks. So be sure to scrape off the old wax ring and inspect the flange. Here are some solutions for broken, corroded or loose flanges:

Ear-type ring

Loose flanges are usually the result of wood rot. The flange screws simply won't hold in the soft, decayed subfloor. The best solution depends on the extent of the rot. If the rot is only under the flange, use an ear-type repair ring. The ears let you drive screws into firm wood farther away from the flange. Before you install this kind of ring, hold it up to the drain horn on the underside of the toilet. You may have to cut off a couple of ears to make it work with your toilet. If the rot extends well beyond the flange, you'll have to replace a section of the subfloor.

Repair ring

Plastic flanges often bend or break, but that's an easy fix. Just screw a stainless steel repair ring over the plastic flange with at least four 1-1/2-in. stainless steel screws. Consider doing this even if the plastic flange is in good shape—it's cheap insurance against future trouble. The repair ring raises the flange by about 1/4 in. So before you install the ring, set it on the flange and set your toilet over it to make sure it fits.

Two-part repair ring

Steel flanges attached to plastic hubs can rust away. The easiest solution is a two-part ring that locks onto the plastic just like the old one. To cut away the old flange, use a hacksaw blade or an angle grinder with a metal-cutting wheel. The repair flange is available at some home centers. To buy online, search for "bay flange."

Repair flange

Cast iron flanges can break or corrode. If only the bolt slot is damaged, slip a repair bracket under the flange. If the flange is in bad shape, you can add a brass repair ring similar to the stainless steel ring shown above or install a plastic flange that slips inside. If necessary, break away the cast iron flange with a cold chisel. Home centers carry one or two slip-in flanges. For a wider variety, search online for "replacement toilet flange."

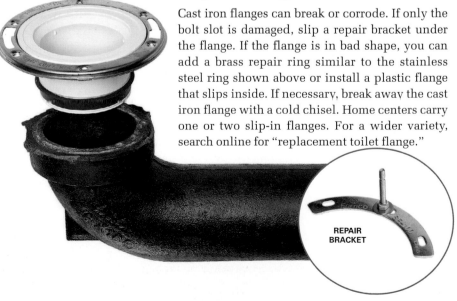

REPAIR BRACKET

Special section: Painting and staining

This special section will help provide the know-how you need to make your painting and staining projects last longer and look more professional. Learn about materials and tools that will make your job go faster, with better results. Get a clearer understanding of the preparation and application methods used by the pros. Find out about storing, setting up, and how to really make finishes stick. Put them all together, and these tips and techniques will help make your project look as great in reality as it does in your imagination.

Learn the art of stenciling.

Speed up cleanups.

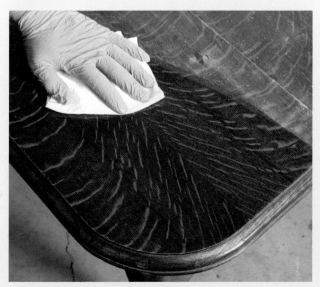
Renew old finishes without stripping.

Learn about new products.

Pro secrets for a speedy, great-looking paint job

Paint twice as fast with this extra-wide roller

An 18-in.-wide roller setup like this may not be for everybody. Painters use them for the obvious reason that they can paint twice as fast as they can with a standard 9-in. roller.

If you have a lot of large, unbroken walls and ceilings, the investment in a large paint pail, 18-in. roller cage and 18-in. cover makes sense for you, too. You'll definitely save a bunch of time. Plus, because the roller is supported on both edges instead of just one, it's easier to apply consistent pressure and avoid roller marks left by paint buildup at the edge of the roller.

You'll find 18-in. roller equipment at most home centers and paint stores.

Prep varnished wood carefully

Every surface should be cleaned before it's painted, but painting over clear finishes like varnish or poly-urethane requires extra care to ensure that the new paint bonds well. Thorough sanding is one way to prepare the surface. But a liquid sander/deglosser is easier and faster.

Read the instructions on the container and follow them carefully. Some types of "liquid sandpaper" require you to paint over them before they dry. Others, like the one we're using, should dry first. Follow the sander/deglosser with a coat of bonding primer. Ask for it at the paint department. Most major paint manufacturers sell it.

Caulk every crack

Rather than trying to decide which cracks are large enough to require caulk, just caulk everything. It's actually faster because you don't have to waste time deciding what to caulk and because you're not constantly starting and stopping. Caulk every intersection between moldings and between moldings and walls or ceilings. You'll be amazed at how much better the final paint job looks when there are no dark cracks showing.

Look for a shed-resistant, woven roller

If you're picky about how your walls look when you're done rolling on the paint, then you'll want a way to avoid leaving a trail of roller fuzzies behind. Look for rollers that are labeled "shed resistant woven." They cost a little more than some covers, but the smooth, lint-free finish is worth it.

Replace your roller tray with a pail

If you're like most homeowners, you have a paint tray that you use to roll walls. And if you've done much painting, you've probably stepped in or spilled the tray at least once. Plus, as you know, trays are awkward to move around, especially when they're fully loaded with paint. A paint pail solves these problems and more. Pails hold more paint than trays, and you'll find them easy to move around and tough to step in! As a bonus, if you use the plastic lining tip we show here, you can practically eliminate cleanup. You'll find paint pails at home centers and paint stores.

1 **Line the pail to simplify cleanup.** Use thin painter's plastic to line the pail. Cut a piece of plastic and drape it into the pail. Add your paint and then run a band of masking tape around the perimeter to hold the plastic in place.

2 **Drain the leftover paint back into the can.** When you're done painting, just bundle up the plastic and pull it out. If there's leftover paint, hold the plastic over your paint can and slit the bottom with a utility knife to drain the paint back into your paint can.

Patch with glazing putty

If you've done much auto body repair, you're probably familiar with glazing putty. On cars, glazing putty is used to fill small scratches and imperfections before painting because it spreads easily and dries quickly and is easy to sand. These same properties also make glazing putty ideal for filling shallow damage in trim. You'll find glazing putty in auto parts stores, hardware stores and some well-stocked paint stores.

A quicker way to mask windows

Unless you're a really good painter, it's quicker to mask window glass than to try to neatly cut in with a brush, especially if you use the masking method we show here. The three photos below show the technique. If you're going to spray-paint the window trim, cover the glass entirely by attaching a piece of paper under the first strip of masking tape. Precut the paper so it's about 1-1/2 in. narrower and shorter than the glass size.

1 Tape both sides of the glass, letting the ends run wild. Push the tape tightly into the corners with a flexible putty knife.

2 Slice off the excess with a utility knife.

3 Finish by taping the top and bottom.

Keep a mini roller and screen handy

A mini roller is great for all kinds of painting tasks. If you fit it with a woven sleeve to match the nap on your large roller, you can use it to touch up and to paint areas where your big roller won't fit.

Buy a small screen and just drop it in your gallon paint can so it'll be handy when you need it. If you use a plastic screen like the one shown, you can push it down into the can and still get the paint can cover on. Then when you need to do a little touch-up, just take off the lid and start rolling. Put a foam cover on your mini roller for painting doors and woodwork.

You'll find a large selection of mini rollers at hardware stores, paint stores and home centers.

Don't start in corners

It's natural to load your brush with paint and stick it into the corner to start painting. But you'll end up with too much paint in the corner, where it's difficult to spread out. Instead, start laying on the paint about 4 to 6 in. from inside corners, and then spread the paint back into the corner with the brush. You'll get a nice, smooth paint job without excess paint buildup at inside corners.

Speedy, accurate masking

The key to perfect masking is to keep the tape straight and tight to the wall. Here's a tip to simplify the job. Stick about 6 in. of tape to the molding. Then, with the tape roll held tight against the wall, unroll about 6 more inches of tape. Rotate the roll down until this section of tape is stuck and repeat the process. The trick is to keep the roll of tape against the wall. It takes a little practice to master this technique, so don't give up. Once you learn to tape this way, your speed and accuracy will increase dramatically.

Fast caulking

A common mistake is to cut off too much of the caulk tube tip, leaving a hole that's way too big for most interior caulking work. When you're filling small cracks to prepare for painting, cut the tip carefully to keep the hole tiny—about 1/16 in. in diameter. The tiny hole lets out just enough caulk to fill typical small- to medium-size cracks.

For larger cracks, make a second pass or keep a second caulk gun on hand, loaded with a tube that has a slightly bigger hole. Keep the caulk gun moving quickly along the crack as you squeeze the trigger. This, combined with the small opening in the tip, will give you a nice caulk joint that needs very little cleanup. A quick swipe with a dampened fingertip will leave a paint-ready joint.

Drop-cloth substitute

Drop cloths can be a hassle. They slip on hard floors, get bunched up under ladders and are difficult to fit tight to baseboards. Eliminate the hassle and save time by using rosin paper instead. You can buy a 160-ft.-long roll of 3-ft.-wide heavy masking paper. Roll it out, leaving about a 1/2-in. space along the wall for the tape. Then cover the edges with tape to keep it in place. You'll find rolls of masking or rosin paper at home centers and paint stores.

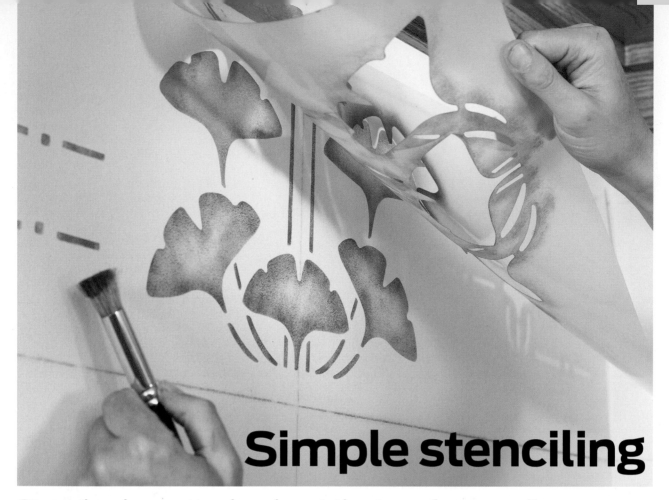

Simple stenciling

Stencil a decorative border at the top of your wall

Stenciling is a traditional decorative technique that perfectly complements many rooms. And it's easy to learn, too. If you can handle a paintbrush and a tape measure, you can quickly master the techniques for applying an attractive, simple border. And with a little practice, you can tackle complex patterns using multiple stencils and colors—and even create your own designs.

The key tools are a special stenciling brush (Photo 2) and the stencil and paint. A wide variety of each are available at craft and art supply stores. You can also find stencil patterns at bookstores or online, or even buy stencil blanks and cut your own with an X-Acto knife. The stencil shown here, a pattern called Ginkgo Frieze, is available online. Match the brush size to the area being filled within the stencil. A 1/2-in., medium-size brush, shown here, is a good, all-purpose size. You can use almost any paint—artist acrylics, wall paints or the special stenciling paints sold at craft and art supply stores. Artist acrylic paint is shown here.

Plan the layout

Position your stencil on the wall at the desired height and mark the alignment holes or top edge. Then snap a light, horizontal chalk line around the room at that height. Make sure that whatever color chalk you use wipes off easily. Or use faint pencil marks, which can be easily removed or covered later.

The key to a good layout is to avoid awkward pattern breaks at doors, windows and corners. To work out the best spacing, measure the stencil pattern and mark the actual repetitions on the wall. Vary the spacing slightly as needed to make the pattern fall in a pleasing way. Or if your stencil has multiple figures, you can alter the spacing between them. Start your layout at the most prominent part of the room and make compromises in less visible areas. Draw vertical lines at the pattern center points to make positioning easier.

Dab on the paint

Tape the stencil pattern on the alignment marks (Photo 1) and put a small quantity of paint on a paper plate. Push the stenciling brush into the paint just enough to coat the tips of the bristles, then pat off the excess on a dry cloth or newspaper, making sure the paint spreads to all the bristles (Photo 2). The brush should be almost dry—remember, it's easier to add paint than it is to take it away.

Lightly dab on the paint (Photo 3). Hold the stencil pattern with your free hand to keep it still and flat.

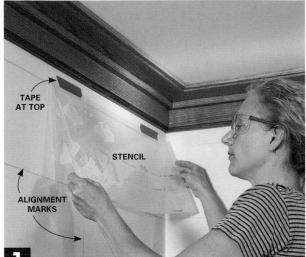

1 Snap lines on the wall to align with the alignment marks on your stencil. Tape the stencil in place along the top edge with removable masking tape.

TAPE AT TOP

STENCIL

ALIGNMENT MARKS

2 Dab the special stenciling brush into the paint, then pat off the bristles on a dry cloth. Leave the brush almost dry.

STENCILING BRUSH

DRY CLOTH

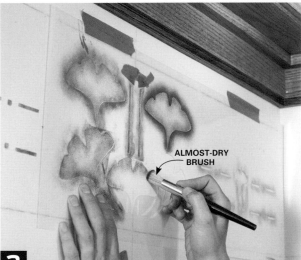

3 Apply the paint to the stencil with light dabbing and swirling motions until the stencil area is covered. Work in from the edges, brushing toward the center.

ALMOST-DRY BRUSH

Don't worry about getting paint on the stencil, but avoid wiping or stabbing too hard around the edges. You can cover the cutout completely or work for shading effects. Cover nearby cutouts with masking tape so you don't accidentally get paint in them (Photo 5).

Mistakes are easy to correct. You can lift the stencil (Photo 4) and wipe off any paint that's smeared under the edge with a damp paper towel, or touch it up later with wall paint. If you wipe some of the stenciled area away, just lay the stencil down again and touch up.

For two colors, mask off the cutout where the second color will go, stencil on the first color all the way around the room, then go back and add the second color, following your original alignment marks (Photo 5). Other colors and even additional stencil patterns can be added in this manner.

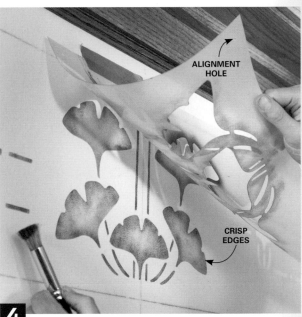

4 Lift the stencil up on the tape hinges and check for paint drips and for clear, sharp edges. Lay the stencil back down and touch up if necessary.

ALIGNMENT HOLE

CRISP EDGES

5 Allow the first color to dry, then tape the stencil up on the same marks and apply the second color. Cover nearby areas of the stencil to avoid getting paint in them.

TAPE PROTECTS FINISHED ART

Refinish furniture without stripping

Less time, less effort, less mess. Better results!

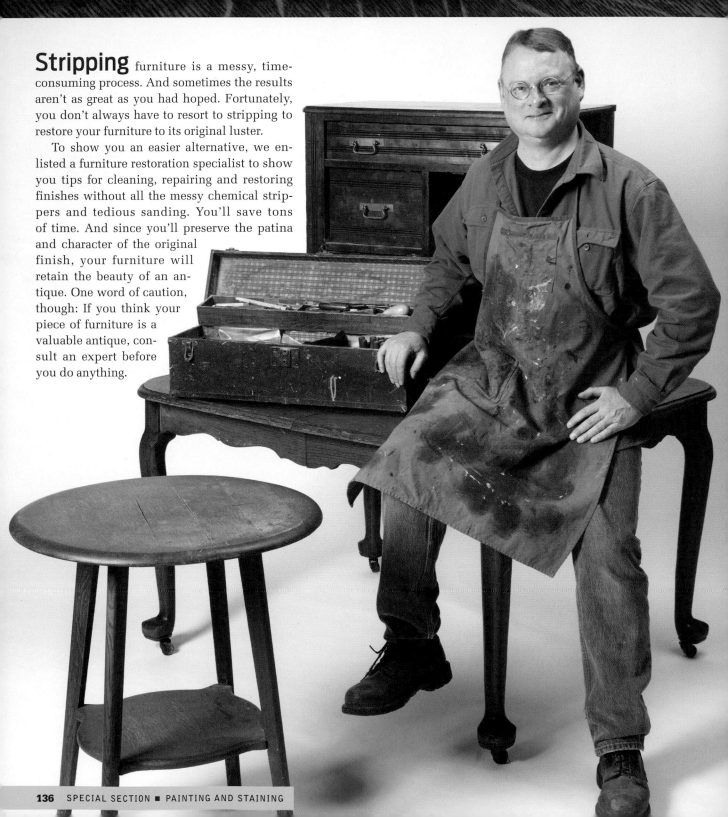

Stripping furniture is a messy, time-consuming process. And sometimes the results aren't as great as you had hoped. Fortunately, you don't always have to resort to stripping to restore your furniture to its original luster.

To show you an easier alternative, we enlisted a furniture restoration specialist to show you tips for cleaning, repairing and restoring finishes without all the messy chemical strippers and tedious sanding. You'll save tons of time. And since you'll preserve the patina and character of the original finish, your furniture will retain the beauty of an antique. One word of caution, though: If you think your piece of furniture is a valuable antique, consult an expert before you do anything.

Assess the finish with mineral spirits

Before you start any repairs or touch-up, wipe on mineral spirits to help you decide what your next steps should be. The mineral spirits temporarily saturates the finish to reveal how the piece of furniture will look with nothing more than a coat of wipe-on clear finish. Don't worry; this won't harm the finish. If it looks good, all you have to do is clean the surface and apply an oil-based wipe-on finish. If the surface looks bad even when wetted with mineral spirits, you'll have to take other measures to restore the finish. We show some of these in the following steps.

Fix white rings

White rings can be easy to get rid of, or they can be a real nightmare. First, slather the ring with petroleum jelly and let it sit overnight. The oil from the petroleum jelly will often penetrate the finish and remove the ring or at least make it less visible.

If that doesn't work, you can try a ring remover (sold at woodworking stores and online). They often work but may change the sheen. If these fixes don't work, consult a pro to see what your other options are.

Clean it up

A thorough cleaning is an important first step in any furniture renewal project. Removing decades of dirt and grime often restores much of the original luster. It's hard to believe, but it's perfectly OK to wash furniture with soap and water.

Our specialist recommends mild liquid dish soap mixed with water. Mix in the same proportion you would to wash dishes. Dip a sponge into the solution, wring it out, and use it to gently scrub the surface. A paintbrush works great for cleaning carvings and moldings. When you're done scrubbing with the soapy water, rinse the surface with a wrung-out sponge and clear water. Then dry it with a clean towel.

Scrape paint without damaging the finish

Paint spatters are common on old furniture, and most of the time you can remove them easily without damaging the finish. Here's a trick for turning an ordinary straightedge razor into a delicate paint scraper. First, wrap a layer of masking tape around each end of the blade, and then bend the blade slightly so it's curved.

The masking tape holds the blade slightly off the surface so you can knock off paint spatters without the blade even touching the wood. Hold the blade perpendicular to the surface. The tape also keeps you from accidentally gouging the wood with the sharp corner of the blade. The curved blade allows you to adjust the depth of the scraper. If you tilt the blade a little, the curved center section will come closer to the surface to allow for removing really thin layers of paint.

Replace missing wood with epoxy

If you discover missing veneer, chipped wood or a damaged molding, you can fix it easily with epoxy putty. Our specialist showed us the process he uses, and the resulting repair is so realistic that it's hard to spot. When it's hardened, the epoxy is light colored and about the density of wood. You can shape, sand and stain it like wood too, so it blends right in. You'll find it at home centers and specialty woodworking stores.

To use this type of epoxy, you slice off a piece with a razor blade or utility knife and knead it in your gloved hand. When the two parts are completely blended to a consistent color and the epoxy putty starts to get sticky, it's ready to use. You'll have about five or 10 minutes to apply the epoxy to the repair before it starts to harden. That's why you should only slice off as much as you can use quickly.

Photo 1 shows how to replace missing veneer. Here are a few things you can do before the putty starts to harden to reduce the amount of sanding and shaping later. First, smooth and shape the epoxy with your finger (Photo 2). Wet it with water first to prevent the epoxy from sticking. Then use the edge of a straightedge razor to scrape the surface almost level with the

surrounding veneer. If you're repairing wood with an open grain, like oak, add grain details by making little slices with a razor while the epoxy is soft (Photo 3).

After the epoxy hardens completely, which usually takes a few hours, you can sand and stain the repair. Stick self-adhesive sandpaper to tongue depressors or craft sticks to make precision sanding blocks (Photo 4) . You can also use spray adhesive or even plain wood glue to attach the sandpaper.

Blend the repair into the surrounding veneer by painting on gel stain to match the color and pattern of the existing grain. You could use stain touch-up markers, but pros prefer gel stain because it's thick enough to act like paint, and can be wiped off with a rag dampened in mineral spirits if you goof up or want to start over.

Choose two colors of stain that match the light and dark areas of the wood. Put a dab of both on a scrap of wood and create a range of colors by blending a bit of the two. Now you can use an artist's brush to create the grain (Photo 5). If the sheen of the patch doesn't match the rest of the wood when the stain dries, you can recoat the entire surface with wipe-on finish to even it out.

1 **Fill the damage with epoxy.** When the epoxy putty is thoroughly mixed, press it into the area to be repaired.

2 **Smooth the putty.** Use your wetted finger to smooth the putty. Press the putty until it's level with the surrounding veneer.

3 **Add wood grain.** On open grain wood like this oak, use a razor blade to add grain marks.

4 **Sand the epoxy.** Sand carefully to avoid removing the surrounding finish. Make a detail sander by gluing sandpaper to a thin strip of wood.

5 **Stain the epoxy to match.** Stain the patch with gel stain to match the color and pattern of the grain. Match the stain color to the light and dark areas of the wood.

Restore the color with gel stain

It's amazing what a coat of gel stain can do to restore a tired-looking piece of furniture. The cool part is that you don't need to strip the old finish for this to work. Our pro demonstrated the tip on this round oak table. The finish was worn and faded. He loaded a soft cloth with dark gel stain and worked it into the surface. Then he wiped if off with a clean cloth. It was a surprising transformation. Of course, gel stain won't eliminate dark water stains or cover bad defects, but it will hide fine scratches and color in areas where the finish has worn away.

There are other products, but gel stain works well because it's easier to control the color and leave a thicker coat if necessary. Also, since it doesn't soak in quite as readily as thinner stains, gel stain is somewhat reversible. Before it dries, you can remove it with mineral spirits if you don't like the results. Gel stains offer some protection, but for a more durable finish or to even out the sheen, let the stain dry overnight and then apply a coat of wipe-on finish as shown below.

Renew the luster with wipe-on finish

The final step in your restoration project is to wipe on a coat of finish. After you clean your furniture piece and do any necessary repairs and stain touch-up, wiping on a coat of finish will restore the sheen and protect the surface. Any wipe-on finish will work. One coat is usually all you need to rejuvenate an existing finish.

To apply wipe-on finish, first put some on a clean rag. Apply it in a swirling motion like you would with car wax. Then wipe off excess finish, going in the direction of the grain. Let the finish dry overnight and you'll be ready to proudly display your furniture restoration project.

Get rid of dents

You can often get rid of small dents by wetting them. The moisture swells the crushed wood fibers back to their original shape. (You can't fix cuts or gouges this way, though.)

Moisture must penetrate the wood for this to work. Finishes prevent water from penetrating, so make a bunch of tiny slits with a razor blade to allow the water to penetrate. Use the corner of the blade, and keep the blade parallel to the grain direction. Next, fill the dent with water and wait until it dries. If the dent is less deep but still visible, you can repeat the process. As with most of the repairs we talk about here, the repaired surface may need a coat of wipe-on finish to look its best.

TIP: Custom-color stain markers

You don't have to settle for a stain touch-up marker that's close enough. Get an exact match by loading a stain marker with the same stain you used on the project. The pen loads like a syringe. Remove the felt tip, stick the end of the pen into the stain, and pull the plunger back to suck stain into the pen. Remember to stir the stain first. Replace the felt tip and you've got a custom-color stain touch-up marker. Search online for "perfect match stain marker."

Fill the stain marker with stain to match your project. Replace the felt tip and you've got a custom-color touch-up marker.

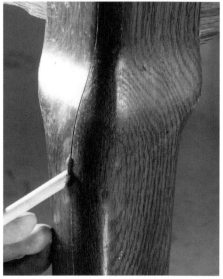

Fill small cracks

If you find nail holes or tiny cracks after applying the final finish, fill them with colored wax fill sticks, wax repair sticks or fill pencils, found at home centers and paint stores.

The directions tell you to rub the stick over the defect. But our pro recommends breaking off a chunk and warming it up in your hands. Then shape it to fit the flaw and press it in with a smooth tool. Use a 3/8-in. dowel with an angle on the end. For cracks, make a thin wafer, slide it into the crack and then work the wax in both directions to fill the crack. Buff with a soft cloth.

7 painting basics

Simple tips for a flawless finish and faster cleanup

1 Set up a staging area

Step one in any painting job is to establish a spot for your stuff. Think through the whole project, gather up all the tools and supplies you'll need and pile them just outside the room. All the gear will be out of your way but within easy reach. And you won't be tripping over it, constantly moving it or hunting for it during the job.

2

Prime every patch

You've filled in the dents and dings, and now it's time to paint, right? Wrong! All those patches, even the tiny ones, must be primed. The unprimed patches will absorb paint and leave noticeable dull spots. This phenomenon is called "flashing," and just like the other type of flashing, it's embarrassing and unprofessional. When you apply primer, don't just brush it on. The tiny ridges of brush marks will show through the paint coat. Instead, "stipple" it on by dabbing your brush against the wall. The bumpy texture will better match the texture of rolled-on paint.

4

Plastic drop cloths lead to paint tracks

Plastic sheets are great for protecting woodwork or furniture, but they're a bad choice for floors. They're slippery on carpet and they don't stay put. Even worse, plastic promotes tracking. That's because spills and drips sit on the surface and dry very slowly, giving you plenty of time to step in the paint and track it around. Fabric, on the other hand, lets paint dry fast, from above and below. Canvas drop cloths are best, but a double layer of old bed sheets works well too.

3

Avoid paint freckles

Rolling paint on the ceiling showers you with a fine mist. A baseball cap is essential and safety glasses let you watch your work without squinting. To make skin cleanup easier, rub lotion on your face, arms and hands. At the end of the day, your paint freckles will wash right off.

5 Overnight storage

If that "quick" painting project didn't go as fast as you'd hoped and you need an extra day, seal your brushes in a freezer bag. As long as it's airtight, you can store brushes for up to a week without cleaning. But don't push it; any longer and they'll dry out and stiffen up, making cleanup that much harder.

6 Wipe down the walls

Static electricity makes dust, lint and even pet hair stick to walls. Rolling paint without cleaning the wall will enshrine them Pompeii-style for all to see. Plus, paint adheres better to clean walls. So wipe down the walls with a damp sponge and warm water before painting. Add a smidgen of dishwashing liquid to the water. A couple of drops is just enough to cut through oil and greasy fingerprints without creating suds that you'll have to wipe off later.

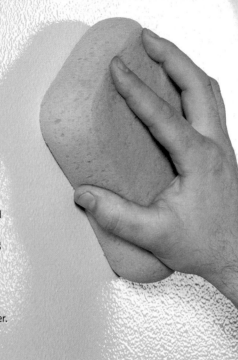

7 Keep a scrapbook

Those labels on paint can lids are like the paint's DNA. They contain all the information needed to duplicate the color and sheen. So the next time you buy paint, ask the clerk to print out a second set of labels and make sure you keep the color chips. Keep them together in a folder so that matching the color later will never be a problem.

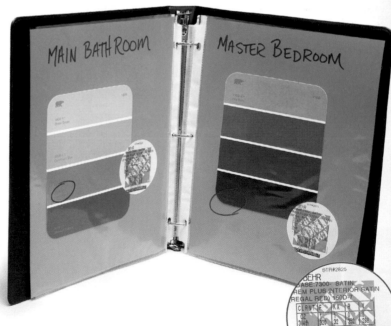

family handyman.com
- There's a right way and a wrong way to do everything—even painting with a roller. Search for "roller tips."
- Thorough prep is the key to a lasting exterior paint job. Search for "paint prep."
- Protect against slop, splatter and spills. Search for "neater painting."

Paint yellowing appliance handles

The white refrigerator in your kitchen didn't come with yellow handles, but they're yellow now. Even after cleaning, they'll still look pretty grungy against the bright white porcelain cabinet. New handles are pretty pricey, so why not just paint them? It's easy and cheap. Buy a can of paint formulated to paint plastic at a home center. Then pick up a bottle of degreaser and a scrubbing pad.

Remove the handles (Photo 1). Then wash them with degreaser and hot water. Use a scrub pad on textured areas to remove the dirt. Pay particular attention to dirt in crevices. Then wipe the handles with a dry cloth and let them air-dry.

Mask off any emblems or chrome trim and paint the handles (Photo 2). Paint the vanity caps at the same time. Then reinstall the handles. You may have to repaint them in a few years. But in the meantime, they'll look a lot better.

1 **Pop the caps and screws.** Pry off the vanity caps that cover the side screws. Then open the fridge door and remove the other screws.

2 **Apply the paint.** Spray the sides of the handles before doing the flat surfaces. Allow the recommended "flash" time before applying additional coats. Let dry, flip them over and paint the other side.

Removing paint drips

Thought you could cut in around wood trim without taping it off, huh? Nice try. Now the paint's dry and you have to remove it. Scraping removes the big blotches but leaves paint in the wood grain. So it's really a two-step process. Start by taping off the wall and removing the largest blotches (Photo 1). Next, scrub off the remaining paint (Photo 2).

1 **Tape and scrape.** Apply painter's tape on the wall to protect the paint. Then apply light pressure to a putty knife and scrape off the surface paint blobs.

2 **Apply paint remover.** Squirt a few drops of paint remover onto an old toothbrush and brush in the direction of the wood grain.